YORK NOTES

THE BRONTËS

SELECTED POEMS

NOTES BY STEVE EDDY

Longman

500012470

York Press

The right of Steve Eddy to be identified as Author
of this Work has been asserted by him in accordance
with the Copyright, Designs and Patents Act 1988

YORK PRESS
322 Old Brompton Road, London SW5 9JH

PEARSON EDUCATION LIMITED
Edinburgh Gate, Harlow,
Essex CM20 2JE, United Kingdom
Associated companies, branches and representatives throughout the world

Quotations from the Brontës' poetry are from *The Brontës: Selected Poems*, edited by Pamela
Norris, 1997, published by Phoenix, a division of the Orion Publishing Group

First published 2008
Second impression 2013
ISBN 978–1–4058–9619–1

Phototypeset by Chat Noir Design, France
Printed in Great Britain

CONTENTS

PART THREE
CRITICAL APPROACHES

PART FOUR
CRITICAL PERSPECTIVES

PART FIVE
BACKGROUND

PART ONE

INTRODUCTION

STUDYING POEMS

Reading poems and exploring them critically can be approached in a number of ways, but when reading a poem for the first time it is a good idea to consider some, or all, of the following:

- **Format and style**: how do poems differ from other genres of text? Does the poem capture a single moment in time, tell a whole story, or make a specific point?

- **The poet's perspective**: consider what the poet has to say, how he or she presents a particular view of people, the world, society, ideas, issues, etc. Are, or were, these views controversial?

- **Verse and metre**: how are stanzas or patterns of lines used to reveal the narrative? What rhythms and rhymes does the poet use to convey an atmosphere or achieve an effect?

- **Choice of language**: does the poet choose to write formally or informally? Does he or she use different registers for different voices in the poem, vary the sound and style, employ literary techniques such as imagery, alliteration and metaphor?

- **Links and connections**: what other texts does this poem remind you of? Can you see connections between its narrative, main characters and ideas and those of other texts you have studied? Is the poem part of a literary tradition or movement?

- **Your perspective and that of others**: what are your feelings about the poem? Can you relate to its emotions, themes and ideas? What do others say about the poem – for example, critics or other poets and writers?

These York Notes offer an introduction to the Brontës' poetry and cannot substitute for close reading of the text and the study of secondary sources.

CHECK THE BOOK

The Cambridge Companion to the Brontës (CUP, 2003) is a good place to start. It is a complete guide to the Brontës, with a chapter on their poetry by Angela Leighton.

READING THE BRONTËS' POETRY

CONTEXT

Jane Eyre and *Villette* were partly based on Charlotte's experiences as a governess and teacher, in England and in Brussels. The portrayal of the drunken and morally degenerate husband in Anne's *The Tenant of Wildfell Hall* is thought to have been influenced by their brother Branwell's behaviour.

CONTEXT

The sisters deliberately published their poems under names which were not obviously female in order to avoid being dismissed by critics.

There are two obvious factors which make studying the Brontës' poetry a rather specialised pursuit – different, say, from studying the poems of Wordsworth or Tennyson. The first is that, with the exception of Branwell, they are far better known as novelists, Charlotte for her semi-autobiographical *Jane Eyre* (1847) and *Villette* (1853), Emily for her highly original *Wuthering Heights* (1847), and Anne for her rather underrated *The Tenant of Wildfell Hall* (1848). *Jane Eyre* was a commercial success immediately, while *Wuthering Heights* appalled some critics at the time and only later came to achieve the towering reputation it has now. *The Tenant of Wildfell Hall* drew some attention, although critics tended to misconstrue its moral purpose and accuse it of being coarse or 'unladylike'.

Despite their fame as novelists, the sisters were, in fact, first published as poets, under the names of Currer, Ellis and Acton Bell, in their 1846 *Poems*. The book was largely ignored, but seeing themselves in print encouraged the sisters to persist with their writing of fiction. Their subsequent establishment as novelists makes them unique in nineteenth-century English literature. Neither Wordsworth nor Tennyson ever wrote a novel; nor did any of the other great exponents of fiction, such as Charles Dickens or Charlotte Brontë's friend Mrs Gaskell, turn their hand to poetry. We therefore have an unusual opportunity in the Brontës to compare their treatment of themes, and autobiographical material, in two quite different literary forms.

Were it not for the sisters' reputations as novelists, their poetry might now be overlooked – with the possible exception of Emily, who is widely regarded as the poetic genius of the family. Moreover, Branwell, who never attempted a full-length novel – probably lacking the emotional and literary self-discipline to do so – would almost certainly be forgotten.

This brings us to the second of the two factors making study of the Brontës' poems unusual – namely, that it involves four siblings who shared a literary gift, a unique phenomenon in the history of English literature. Close in age, motherless, and with relatively few external influences for at least some of their childhood years, they influenced each other deeply, both emotionally and imaginatively. This has led many commentators to approach them as a single literary phenomenon rather than as four separate individuals.

A major factor in the early literary development of all four children was their creation of vivid fantasy worlds partly inspired by a set of toy soldiers which their father gave to Branwell. The children made up plays, and then, when Charlotte was about ten, began to write stories about the characters that featured in them. Charlotte and Branwell made up the imaginary worlds of Glasstown, then Angria; Emily and Anne invented Gondal. These were worlds of high drama – love, hate, revenge, power struggles, persecution and betrayal. Most importantly for a study of the Brontës' verse, all four siblings continued to write poems relating to their epics well into adult life. This is especially true of the best poet among them – Emily – for whom the fiercely individualistic world of Gondal remained a fitting expression of her personality.

> **CHECK THE BOOK**
> The Angria and Gondal epics were written in minute script in tiny books. Although some of the Angrian stories survive (see Charlotte Brontë, *Tales of Angria*, Penguin Classics, 2006), the Gondal tales have been lost. They were reconstructed from the poetry by Laura L. Hinkley, in *The Brontës* (1947).

Although the sisters removed many of the overt references to Angria and Gondal when they prepared their poems for publication in 1846, there are many poems in the Everyman collection in which the Angrian or Gondalian contexts are still clear, especially among those by Emily. For example, 'To a Wreath of Snow by A. G. Almeda' is narrated by Augusta Almeda, Queen of Gondal, from the dungeon where she is imprisoned, and 'F. De Samara to A. G. A.' is Fernando de Samara's bitter suicide note to Augusta. Even Emily's best-known poem, 'Remembrance', was originally called 'R. Alcona to J. Brenzaida', and is Rosina Alcona's lament for her assassinated lover, the tyrannical but glorious Julius Brenzaida – who later metamorphosed into Heathcliff in *Wuthering Heights*.

Although Emily and Anne collaborated on the Gondal stories and almost certainly influenced each other's poetry, Anne's mature poems – among which are those in this collection – are mostly explorations of her own feelings, sometimes inspired by nature – and of her religious doubts and convictions. She may have come to

CONTEXT

The exotic names of the Gondal characters reflect their natures but also detach them from the restraints of everyday reality, in the way that Italian names and settings did for the characters of such Shakespeare plays as *The Merchant of Venice*. It is also a feature of some gothic writing to remove the setting to an exotic country. See, for example, Ann Radcliffe's *The Italian* (1797).

CONTEXT

Branwell's 'Now – but one moment, let me stay' may relate to the Battle of Evesham (1265), fought between Simon de Montfort and Prince Edward, since it refers to 'Evesham's woody brow'. Branwell's interest in medieval history is also found in his poem 'Penmaenmawr'.

shun the amoral world of Gondal as she became more devoutly Christian. As for Charlotte, she was at her best as a poet when writing directly about her own experience and emotions, and this is perhaps why the Everyman collection contains no obviously Angrian poems by Charlotte. 'Retrospection', however, describes the 'web' of fantasy that she and her siblings wove, and both the gothic 'Mementos' and the atmospheric 'Early wrapt in slumber deep' have a narrative voice that relates to her Angrian storytelling. A few of the poems by Branwell included in the edition have an Angrian context. 'Augusta' is spoken by Branwell's fictional hero Alexander Percy, Earl of Northangerland, to his first wife, Augusta di Segovia. 'On Caroline' may be partly Angrian, and 'Now – but one moment, let me stay', in which the speaker enjoys a moment of peace before joining a battle, certainly sounds Angrian, even if it is actually based on a real medieval battle.

How one regards the importance of Angria and Gondal in the poetry – especially in the case of Emily – is very much a matter of personal interpretation. Some critics have made a distinction between Emily's Gondal and non-Gondal poems, citing the fact that she recorded them in separate notebooks. However, in reality, the line is blurred. While it would be a mistake to think that 'Remembrance' was directly related to an actual bereavement suffered by Emily, few readers would question the power of the emotion it expresses: it is not simply an imaginative contrivance. It also explores themes – of loss and memory – which feature in non-Gondal poems such as 'The bluebell is the sweetest flower'. Writing in the voice of a Gondal persona may give Emily a freedom to write about emotions which it would be difficult to express more directly, as well as allowing her to contemplate taboo subjects such as suicide in 'F. De Samara to A. G. A'. In addition, the Gondal narrative may provide a convenient symbolic framework for her ideas, as in 'The Prisoner, a fragment', in which a young woman's imprisonment in a dungeon symbolises the soul's imprisonment within the body. The blurred line between Gondal and non-Gondal can be seen in the fact that she explores similar ideas in the non-Gondal poem 'Stars'.

It is not essential to understand the Gondal context of Emily's poems in order to appreciate them. In fact it is now impossible to relate the poems exactly to the stories, as they have been lost. However, it does help our understanding of these poems if we are aware of the kind of larger-than-life characters that populate and narrate them. In the case of Branwell's Angrian poems, the situation is a little more straightforward. Branwell identified closely with his principal Angrian hero Percy, the speaker in 'Augusta', and in most of his poems he is his own hero. Even in 'On Caroline', which reads as if it had a narrative context but which may reflect the loss of his beloved older sister Maria, he turns from contemplation of the dead woman to the romantically bereft figure that he strikes himself. 'Epistle From a Father to a Child in Her Grave' shows the same self-preoccupied tendency. It has been suggested that this poem has an Angrian context, but Juliet Barker makes a convincing case for it being addressed to Branwell's own deceased illegitimate child. Whichever is the case, the poem largely expresses Branwell's sense of his own suffering.

Given the formative creative background of the Brontë siblings, their shared literary influences, and the amount of time they spent together even in later years, it is not surprising that they show similarities of theme and style. Being aware of these similarities can add a depth to any study of their poems. At the same time it can point up their individual strengths, weaknesses and concerns. Thematically, the most important shared feature of their poems is a preoccupation with loss in various forms. Psychologically speaking, this might stem from the loss of their mother in 1821, as well as their sisters Maria and Elizabeth within almost a month of each other in 1825.

The most obvious form of loss is bereavement, and this is the subject of a number of poems in the collection. Charlotte's 'Mementos' tells the story of a woman who dies heartbroken, and her poems on the deaths of Emily and Anne are among her finest. Branwell's 'On Caroline' and 'Epistle From a Father to a Child in Her Grave' are laments, as are Emily's 'A Death-Scene' and 'Remembrance', among others, and Anne's 'A Reminiscence'. Less obviously, there are the poems about lost childhood innocence and delight, such as Charlotte's 'Retrospection', Branwell's 'Death Triumphant', and Anne's 'Memory'. It also speaks of the close bond

CHECK THE BOOK

Juliet Barker's *The Brontës* (Phoenix Press, 1994) is widely regarded as the most comprehensive and insightful biography on the whole family.

CHECK THE POEM

Lost childhood innocence was a theme for some of the Romantic poets, too, notably William Wordsworth. In his 'Intimations of Immortality', he regrets 'That there hath past away a glory from the earth' since he left childhood behind.

CONTEXT

Pantheism, the belief that the divine, or God, is to be found throughout nature, finds expression to varying degrees in a number of Romantic poets, especially Wordsworth, Coleridge and Shelley. More recently, Ted Hughes (1930–98) has identified nature with a universal force both of creation and destruction. See especially his *Crow* (1970).

shared by the siblings, especially the sisters, that all three sisters write about homesickness and missing their family in a number of poems, for example Charlotte's 'The Teacher's Monologue', Emily's 'Loud without the wind was roaring', and Anne's 'Home'.

The siblings seem to have found it difficult to form relationships outside of the family. The three sisters were shy, and the most outgoing of them, Charlotte, regarded herself as far too plain for any man to love her, as revealed in 'He saw my heart's woe'. Anne writes in 'Dreams' of the married life she never managed to find. Even Branwell, though charming, was depressive and emotionally fragile. His only significant romantic relationship was an affair with his employer's wife, and his grief at its ending is commemorated in 'Penmaenmawr'.

All four siblings, too, express in their various ways a spiritual yearning – perhaps not least because of having a church minister for a father. Often, this yearning is coupled with a tendency to regard earthly life as a time of unavoidable suffering, characterised by frequent use of words such as 'drear', 'dreary', 'anguish' and 'despair'. Charlotte consoles herself for earthly loneliness and loss with the promise of the conventional Christian heaven, while Anne yearns more fervently for union with God. Branwell, who declared himself an atheist, seems to turn to God in some of his later poems, such as 'O God! while I in pleasure's wiles' (1846). Emily, on the other hand, rejects conventional religion completely: 'Vain are the thousand creeds/ That move men's hearts, unutterably vain' ('No Coward Soul is Mine'). Instead she pursues her own mystical vision of wholeness, as in 'Stars' and 'The Prisoner'. Like Anne, she is often inspired by nature, but whereas this inspiration leads Anne to God, it leads Emily towards a form of pantheism, or nature worship. If Emily does not quite worship nature, then she at least regards it as an expression of the divine. However, at times she also suggests that she must ultimately give it up in order to achieve a higher level of spirituality. (See 'Stars' and 'The Night-Wind', and **Themes: Spiritual yearning**.)

Stylistically the four siblings also had a certain amount in common. They shared a formality, a preference for regular metre and rhyme, and a tendency, already mentioned, to overuse words such as 'drear' and 'dreary'. Charlotte, Emily and Branwell were drawn towards the gothic, and its preoccupation with dungeons, ghosts and the decaying past as evidence of the transience of life. They all have a liking for personification of abstract ideas. Emily, for example, manages five such abstractions in one poem, 'Imagination': Imagination itself, Reason, Nature, Truth and Fancy. In this the Brontës followed Romantic poets such as Keats and Shelley.

On the other hand, the siblings were individuals. Charlotte is perhaps the most addicted to self-consciously 'poetic' language and archaisms, and to overly regular metres, yet she sometimes expresses her deepest feelings very movingly. Anne's language has a simple eloquence and fervour. Branwell, though often egotistical, writes at best with a sense of grandeur and a painter's eye for visual detail. Emily, above all, writes with a musical sense of the cadences of language, and with a subtlety of expression that makes her rise above her siblings to the ranks of the greatest English poets.

CHECK THE BOOK

Jane Eyre and *Wuthering Heights* both have strong gothic elements. The former features an ancestral mansion that harbours a dark secret, while the latter combines subjection and the supernatural.

CHECK THE POEM

One classic example of Romantic **personification** of abstract ideas is 'Ode on Melancholy', by John Keats (1795–1821). He writes: 'She dwells with Beauty – Beauty that must die;/ And Joy, whose hand is ever at his lips/ Bidding adieu; and aching Pleasure nigh.'

PART TWO

THE TEXT

NOTE ON THE TEXT

The poems in the Everyman edition, ed. Pamela Norris (1997), which has been used in these Notes, are selected from *Poems* by Currer, Ellis and Acton Bell (London, 1846).

DETAILED SUMMARIES

CHARLOTTE BRONTË

FROM RETROSPECTION

- The poet reflects on how her childhood fantasy world has flowered.
- She comments on how important this world of the imagination is to her now.

The poet recalls the fantasy world that she created with her siblings in childhood, asks what has become of it, and then answers her own question. Far from having faded, she says, it has developed in adulthood, flowering into something greater. She reflects, too, on how her continuing awareness of this imaginative 'dream' has sustained her in the darker times of her young adulthood, even when far away from her family home.

COMMENTARY

Charlotte commences with four metaphors for the imaginative inspiration shared by herself and her three siblings. The number of metaphors probably corresponds to the number of children, though there is no obvious individual correspondence. It is appropriate that these metaphors are taken from the natural world: a web, a spring, a mustard seed and an almond branch. The first two are ascribed the

CONTEXT

The mustard seed in 'Retrospection' (line 5) alludes to a biblical parable: 'Then said he, Unto what is the kingdom of God like? And whereunto shall I resemble it? It is like a grain of mustard seed, which a man took, and cast into his garden; and it grew, and waxed a great tree; and the fowls of the air lodged in the branches of it' (Luke 13:18–19). It is also given, in a different form, in Mark 4:30–2 and Matthew 13:31–2.

characteristics of youthful innocence: 'sunny air' (2) and 'water pure and fair' (4), while the second two allude to the biblical parable of the mustard seed and to the Old Testament story of Aaron's rod. Given Charlotte's religious feelings, we can see that these allusions point to what she saw as the holy nature of this childhood inspiration. The rhythm and simple rhyme scheme of these lines also match the simplicity of childhood.

The third stanza takes the same form as the first two but it introduces a darker note, and a question. Life – for Charlotte even at the age of nineteen – is now 'darkly shaded' (11), and childhood joys are fast disappearing. She asks whether the tokens of childhood imagination have also disappeared. In stanza 4, however, she dismisses this idea with the exclaimed 'Faded!' (13). The web of their childhood imaginings still has a certain insubstantiality, being 'of air' (13), but it has grown, and now has the rich colouring of an Italian sunset – suggesting that it has broadened with the horizons of its creators. This stanza itself has an extra three lines, and a final line rhyming with its fourth line, both suggesting a new level of sophistication in Charlotte and her siblings.

The fifth stanza is even longer and seems to cast new doubt on the survival of the original inspiration. However, Charlotte again dismisses this doubt, with the admonition 'Hark! sceptic bid thy doubts be gone' (22). The spring, rather grandiosely, has turned into an entire sea (which the phrase 'feeble roar' rather feebly describes, 23), and the 'armed fleets' (25) riding upon it strongly suggest the epic fantasy world of Angria. This sea is huge – not quite the infinite sea of Emily's poems (see, for example, 'Stars'), but still impressive. In the next stanza we find that the other metaphors – the mustard seed and the almond-wand – have also flourished. Even the almond tree, despite an unpromising start, has defied expectations, just as new life springs each year from the apparently dead heath (35).

Charlotte then directly addresses the childhood inspiration ('Dream that stole o'er us', 39). The whole of the penultimate stanza is grammatically one sentence, bringing the poem to what is intended to be a swelling climax. In essence, she says that the dream that possessed the siblings as children does so even more as they

CONTEXT

The almond rod in 'Retrospection' relates to 'Aaron's sceptre', which in turn alludes to the Old Testament story given in Numbers 17:8, in which Moses left a stave from each tribe of the Israelites in the Tabernacle overnight. His brother Aaron's stave had budded and produced ripe almonds. Aaron, perhaps significantly, was a better speaker than Moses, and therefore became his spokesman.

 CHECK THE POEM

The image of new life springing from the dead heath in 'Retrospection' is reminiscent of Emily's 'Loud without the wind was roaring'.

approach maturity (indicated by Sirius, the Dog Star, most visible in high summer). Speaking for herself, she observes that, as the scenes of imagination protect her from the worst of the 'cold world's darkest features' (46), she has ever more respect for the 'god-like creatures' (48) of her imagination – and perhaps specifically those which people Angria.

After this climactic, though rather confusing, stanza, the final one comes almost as an afterthought. Charlotte is presumably referring to her lonely times in Roe Head School, through which she was sustained by the world of imagination built up from her childhood. All four lines rhyme, perhaps to give the poem a sense of completion. However, the effect is rather pedestrian, especially coupled with the awkward scansion. This is produced by the second line, in which the sense demands that we stress 'round', while the rhythm stresses 'me', and by the extra two syllables included in the final line.

GLOSSARY	
40	vernal clime springtime (more literally, spring climate)
44	Sirius the Dog Star, brightest in August

CHECK THE POEM

Charlotte's interest in ghosts is in tune with her general interest in the **gothic** genre. Her poem 'Mementos' is gothic in its concern with a decaying past, represented not least in its narrator's fear of seeing '**Some shape that should be well in heaven,/ Or ill elsewhere**' (39–40) as she climbs the stairs.

'THE AUTUMN DAY ITS COURSE HAS RUN'

- The poet takes a gloomy comfort in the twilight, which resembles the ghostly presence of a nun.

The poet comments on the stealthy advance of the autumn evening twilight. She personifies the twilight as if it were a ghostly nun whom she invites to accompany her at her fireside.

COMMENTARY

This fragment, written in Brussels, probably in 1845, is mostly notable for the atmosphere it creates, and for its touching on two of Charlotte's preoccupations: her own loneliness and the supernatural – a common feature of the gothic genre. It is unusual for Charlotte in its long lines and use of internal rhymes and half-rhymes. The first two lines could in theory even be arranged as follows:

> The Autumn day its course has run –
> The Autumn evening falls;
> Already risen, the Autumn moon
> Gleams quiet on these walls

We see the half-rhyme of 'run' and 'moon' and the full internal rhymes of 'gloom … room' (4) and 'spread … shed' (5). These perhaps achieve a certain sense of harmony, suggestive of the feeling experienced by Charlotte at the end of a day's teaching.

Although the fragment is short, it creates a powerful atmosphere. The moon quietly gleaming provides a sense of focus. The twilight, personified as a ghostly nun, is given added mystery by being announced simply as 'a silent guest' (3), its silence being in tune with that of the moon. The personification is hinted at by the phrase 'Her veil is spread' (5) before it is named outright as 'silent Nun' (7).

Line 4 is especially effective in creating atmosphere, with the rhyming of 'gloom' and 'room', together with the interesting use of 'dusk' as an adjective and its effective alliterative coupling with 'dumb'. The twilight seems almost to metamorphose into the imagined nun, a fitting confidante for Charlotte, who saw herself as destined to be lonely and unloved.

'EARLY WRAPT IN SLUMBER DEEP'

- The poet describes a sleeping household and its surroundings on a moonlit summer night.

In this unusually restrained poem, Charlotte simply describes the inhabitants of a house sleeping soundly through a summer night.

CHECK THE POEM
A more modern poem in which the moon creates atmosphere and provides a focus is Philip Larkin's 'Sad Steps' (*High Windows*, Faber, 1974).

CONTEXT
Bettina Knapp in *The Brontës: Branwell, Anne, Emily, Charlotte* (Continuum, 1992) conjectures that the myths that the young Brontës wove, and the subsequent fictional and poetic narratives, may have influenced their actual lives as much as their lives influenced their work. By this way of thinking, Charlotte may have been doomed to being rejected romantically because of her tragic fantasies.

CHECK THE BOOK

Charlotte's political novel *Shirley* portrays poor workers with sympathy, although it condemns violent industrial action and largely upholds the status quo.

She touches on the various representatives of the social spectrum – from the servant to the master – and paints an impressionistic picture of the house and its surroundings.

COMMENTARY

This poem may be unfinished as it appears to be setting a scene – and rather beautifully – perhaps for a longer narrative. Unlike most of Charlotte's other poems, there is no moral argument or conclusion, and no obvious emotional burden. If there is a theme it is in the implied connection between sleep and the passing of time.

Although Charlotte was not a political radical, there is a certain sense of social levelling in her description of the various representatives of the social hierarchy, 'serving-men;/ Master, dame, and hand-maid' (2–3) within the house and 'little herd-boy' (12) in an outdoor shed, all united by the same human need for sleep.

They are 'Early wrapt' (1), suggesting that it is still early in the night. This means that although it is summer, the night will remain for several hours yet, which adds to the sense of peace. This is complemented by the sense of well-being conveyed by their sleeping 'Sound, at Bonny glen' (4).

CHECK THE POEM

Ralph Waldo Emerson wrote in his poem 'Concord Hymn' (1836): 'And Time the ruined bridge has swept/ Down the dark stream that seaward creeps.'

Charlotte is not the first poet to have imaged time as a 'dark stream' (5), but the metaphor is effective here and contrasts with the moonlit brightness of the actual brook in the final stanza. A similarly pleasing comparison is found in the 'drapery' (9) (presumably a curtain) falling over each window and the 'Shade' (10) which spreads over the eyes of the sleepers.

We move from the sleeping house to the seemingly wide-awake night. The moon casts a 'Splendid light' (13). The dewy fields appear to smile in response, reflecting the moon's light 'clear as noon' (15). Whereas the stream of time 'Glides' (6), the real brook 'flows/ Fast, with trembling brightness' (18), full of vibrant life. Significantly, the poem ends with the brightly shining 'silver' road (20), a symbol of potential and opportunity.

GLOSSARY

4	**Bonny** attractive, healthy (Scottish dialect)
	glen a secluded highland valley, especially in Scotland
16	**lea** meadow

'HE SAW MY HEART'S WOE'

- The poet recalls being spurned by a man she loved, and turns to God as a more reliable comfort.

In this poem of rejected love, the poet describes a man's awareness of her desperate need for his love, her eventual confession of her feelings, and his complete lack of response. She goes on to describe her own anguish in the face of this rejection, and to call on God to comfort her.

COMMENTARY

This is a poem of heartfelt emotion, albeit clumsily expressed at times and rather unconvincing in its conclusion. Charlotte is almost certainly writing about her unrequited love for her teaching colleague and mentor Constantin Heger, with whom she worked in Brussels. Being of a religious temperament, Charlotte compares her adoration of Heger with the worship of the Middle Eastern deity Baal. She probably had in mind the biblical story of the Israelites being tempted away from worship of Yahweh by the cult of Baal. The Israelites are also said to have worshipped stone idols, and in this poem Charlotte portrays Heger as 'an idol cut in rock' (13), a 'Granite God' (15) and as her 'Baal' (16). The implication is that the suffering caused by her being rejected is deserved because she has strayed from the true God and become an 'Idolater' (13). However, one may well regard this as a rather desperate attempt to reconcile herself to rejection.

There is also a confusion of feeling in her description of Heger. In the light of rejection, she attempts to cast her beloved in a less

? QUESTION

Do you think that the violent image of self-harm in 'slashed my flesh and drawn my heart's best blood' points to a certain underlying anger in the poet, or to self-pity? Or is she simply pointing up her beloved's lack of response?

CHECK THE POEM

The consolation that Charlotte takes in Emily's escape from life's woes may be compared with Branwell's 'Peaceful Death and Painful Life', which asks 'Why dost thou sorrow for the happy dead?/ For if their life be lost, their toils are o'er' (1–2).

favourable light, as rather heartless, 'spirit-blind' to her anguish (4), unsympathetically standing 'stirless as a tower' (9), a man of stone both in the sense of his unresponsiveness and of his being like a stone idol. If she has 'sought love where love was utterly unknown' (12), then this implies that he is a man incapable of love, who would ignore her even if she 'slashed [her] flesh' (14). In reality Heger was a married man, jointly running, with his wife, the pensionnat where Charlotte taught. He had every reason to reject her. The shame which leads to her self-exile (stanza 5) in part acknowledges her own fault.

The last three stanzas are really a prayer. Charlotte grovels in humiliation as one of the 'suffering worms' (24) before the throne of God, pleading for healing, forgiveness and comfort, and comparing the stony-hearted Heger with the Christian God of compassion. In the final two stanzas she moves away from a close focus on her own suffering, to an all-encompassing statement of her faith in the Christian God to offer comfort to all believers.

> **GLOSSARY**
>
> 16   Baal A Semitic word originally meaning simply 'lord' or 'owner', which is used more specifically in the Old Testament (for example, Judges 8:33) to denote a deity for whom the Israelites for a time forsook Yahweh

ON THE DEATH OF EMILY JANE BRONTË

- The poet speaks of the grief of losing her sister.
- She takes comfort in the fact that Emily's suffering is ended, and looks forward to meeting her in heaven.

The poet describes the terrible grief that she, Anne and their father have felt at Emily's death, and consoles herself with the fact that Emily herself will never know this pain. Bearing this in mind, she says they will not wish for Emily's return. More broadly, she comments that to live is to mourn, and asks God to help them through their grief and eventually unite the family again in heaven.

COMMENTARY

This poem is dated Christmas Eve 1848, just five days after Emily's death. The fact that Charlotte has the self-discipline to express her grief so movingly and in such a balanced and poetically well-formed manner is perhaps partly due to Emily's long illness, in that both Charlotte and Anne had been expecting Emily's death for some time. Hence the poem conveys a sense of an enduring grief rather than just the immediate pain of a sudden bereavement. The poem's rhythm and rhyme scheme work well, avoiding Charlotte's occasional fault of twisting lines awkwardly merely to fit a prescribed pattern. The expression of grief is powerful, yet there is a dignified restraint which avoids overstatement.

In the first three stanzas of the poem, Charlotte expresses the grief borne by both her and her family – her father and Anne (Branwell having died in September of that year). At the same time she is expressing relief that Emily will never know this grief. The language she uses is entirely appropriate: 'grinding agony' (2) and 'nightly anguish' (7) evoke the long lead-up to Emily's death, as well as the anticipation of grieving yet to come. The phrase 'crushing truth' (8) suggests the heavy weight of renewed realisation as the bereaved awake and remember their loss.

The use of imagery is restrained but effective. Agony is 'grinding' (2), like a mill wheel ever turning. The bereaved 'tear' consolation (4), suggesting the sense of the loved one being violently torn from them. Grief is like an arrow piercing the already bitter ('galled') heart (10). Life is a 'lone wilderness' (15), a **metaphor** which would have appealed to Emily herself, but which especially expresses Charlotte's view of life as a very lonely affair.

The final stanza is a far more convincing conclusion than is found in 'He saw my heart's woe'. Charlotte takes comfort in Emily being spared pain, and then stoically comments on the inevitability of human suffering: 'He that lives must mourn' (21). The last three lines are a quiet prayer – not the great chest-beating appeal that we

CHECK THE POEM

In 'Lines: Far away is the land of rest', Emily herself pictures life as a **'dreary road'** (10) on which the traveller carries **'life's tiresome load'** (12) until he finally reaches **'the land of rest'** (20). Similarly, in her 'Stanzas', the **narrator** expresses her weariness with life and her desire to end it.

find at the end of 'He saw my heart's woe'. In a final image, Charlotte looks forward to reaching their common 'bourne' (24), perhaps sensitively avoiding a more explicit description of heaven, since Emily's conception of the afterlife was less conventionally Christian than her own.

The form of this poem is slightly unusual for Charlotte: six-line stanzas, largely in pentameter, with each third line consisting of three feet instead of four (that is, being two syllables shorter than the preceding two lines). This gives a sense of curtailment which corresponds to the cutting off of Emily's life. The rhyme scheme of *aabccb* neatly links the two three-line sections of each stanza. Each of these is a complete sentence, and the final rhyme of each stanza adds to the sense of curtailment already produced by the shortening of lines 3 and 6.

GLOSSARY

24	bourne archaic word for destination

CHECK THE POEM

'On the Death of Anne Brontë' is an understandably bleak poem. Its sentiments are very much in contrast with the rather forced cheerfulness of Charlotte's 'Life', in which she asks 'What though Death at times steps in,/ And calls her best away?'

ON THE DEATH OF ANNE BRONTË

- The poet reflects on losing a second sister, and on her own bleak prospects.

Charlotte simply states that she has little desire to live now that Anne is dead. She reflects on what it was like watching Anne's decline, longing for her suffering to end, then thanking God for ending it. In the final stanza, she anticipates the gloomy, troubled 'weary strife' (16) that is all she can hope for in her life to come.

COMMENTARY

This poem was written just over a month after Anne's death in Scarborough, in 1849. Although poignantly expressing Charlotte's loss, it is calmer in tone than her poem on Emily's death, perhaps reflecting the slightly longer lapse of time before its composition. One must remember too that Charlotte had now lost all three of her siblings to tuberculosis in the space of just over eight months, and one might expect a degree of resignation in her mood.

The poem is also simpler in form than Charlotte's poem on Emily's death, perhaps deliberately echoing the style of Anne's own poetry. The rhyme scheme is a straightforward *abab*, framing the simple sincerity of the feeling, while the metre is iambic except for a slight variation in the first three lines of the second stanza, in which the sense obliges us to stress the opening syllable of each line. This slows the lines down to match Anne's lingering decline and emphasises the opening words: 'Calmly … Wishing … Longing' (1).

The second stanza brings movingly to mind what it was like for Charlotte to sit beside her dying sister day after day, observing her 'failing breath' (5) and hearing her sighs. Death is portrayed as a 'shade' (7), meaning a shadow – but with the added connotation of 'ghost' – as a 'cloud' and as a 'stillness' (9).

In her anticipation of the life to come, there is the same sense of having to struggle on joylessly against adversity as in 'On the Death of Emily Jane Brontë'. There we find 'Weary, weary, dark and drear', and here she sees herself, and presumably her father, as 'benighted' and having to bear 'the weary strife' (15–16). There is the same understandable pessimism, but this time without the sustaining hope of heaven that concludes the earlier poem.

QUESTION

It might be thought that 'On the Death of Anne Brontë' is a better poem than 'On the Death of Emily Jane Brontë', expressing a more genuine feeling, perhaps reflecting a strained relationship between Charlotte and Emily. How do you think the two poems compare?

PATRICK BRANWELL BRONTË

'THE MAN WHO WILL NOT KNOW ANOTHER'

- Branwell says that a man who distances himself from others diminishes himself, and tells his friend Grundy not to behave in this way.
- He adds that he is Grundy's equal.
- Branwell warns Grundy not to behave like him, but to acknowledge his finer feelings nonetheless.

CONTEXT

Francis Grundy wrote of Branwell in *Pictures of the Past*: 'Poor, brilliant, gay, moody, moping, wildly excitable, miserable Brontë! No history records your many struggles after the good, your wit, brilliance, attractiveness, eagerness for excitement – all the qualities which made you such "good company", and dragged you down to an untimely grave.'

CHECK THE POEM

A twentieth-century poem which uses the technique of synecdoche is 'The Hand that Signed the Paper' by Dylan Thomas (1914–53) in which Thomas writes: 'The hand that signed the paper felled a city;/ Five sovereign fingers taxed the breath,/ Doubled the globe of dead and halved a country.'

This poem appears to be a gentle reprimand to Branwell's friend Francis Grundy for ignoring him, although in its original form it may have been more general in its purpose. The poet comments on the kind of man who lacks compassion towards others. He warns Grundy against behaving distantly and tells him not to think it beneath him to acknowledge anyone who approaches him courteously, since even the poorest man is his fellow human being, and Branwell himself is his equal. He warns Grundy against emulating his own behaviour, but insists that he has finer points, too, including being a loyal friend.

COMMENTARY

This cautionary poem falls somewhere between a noble appeal for universal compassion and a slightly petulant personal complaint by one who feels himself snubbed. It begins in sweeping, universal mode, the first three lines building up effectively to the dire fate of the man who lacks compassion. Branwell uses the rhetorical technique of synecdoche, making the part stand for the whole, in 'His frozen eye, his bloodless heart' (5), and personifies Nature as finding this man 'repugnant' (6).

The sense of universal appeal is somewhat undermined by the personal address to 'Grundy' (7), and after the first stanza the poem becomes more personal. Although the warning is phrased eloquently enough, its abstract terms – 'nobler aim' (7), 'shame' (8), 'courtesy' (10), 'gentle birth' (12) – make the poem seem rather dry. The couplet at the start of the third stanza is a succinct and effective statement of the equality of man, but the stanza ends less felicitously. One wonders why Branwell chose the phrase 'worn and dead' (17), unless it was to rhyme with 'head' (18). The glittering light presumably suggests a halo.

In the final stanza, Branwell presumably refers, rather incongruously, to his own 'tottering limbs' (19). Perhaps he is implying drunkenness, especially since he warns his friend to 'shun his evil ways' (21). The second half of the stanza is touching, however. Branwell makes claims for his own inner nobility, thoughtfulness and compassion, and, in the poem's last simple phrase, his loyalty to Grundy.

ON CAROLINE

- The narrator mourns the passing of his wife and insists that he will never forget her.

The narrator, addressing himself in the second person (the 'thee' of line 9), speaks of the death of his wife (his 'borrowed bride', 32). She was evidently a woman of high rank, who lived in a palace (which is perhaps also the 'ancestral hall' referred to by the narrator in line 1), and is now buried in a 'minster' (4) – a major church, like York Minster. He recalls her death bed, and despairs of ever finding happiness without her. He says he will never recover from her death.

COMMENTARY

The dignified language and stately iambic metre of this requiem convey a fitting sense of gravitas. The opening stanza establishes the tone, since it takes the whole stanza to say, in several different ways, that Caroline is dead. Its use of personification ('Eternal sleep' and 'peace and pleasure made their shrine', 5–6), as elsewhere in the poem, adds to a sense of formality. It also uses synecdoche (as in 'The man who will not know another') very effectively to say how death has replaced life:

> She has changed her palace for a pall,
> Her garden walks for minster aisles. (3–4)

The alliteration of 'palace … pall' and the neat comparison with 'garden walks' and 'minster aisles' (in which the living, or perhaps the ghostly dead, might also walk) heightens the sense of contrast between life and death. The reference to her 'golden head' (7) recalls her living beauty, and the final line of the stanza leaves us in no doubt about the speaker's feelings.

The second stanza is rather gothic, focusing on Caroline's death bed and on a sense of darkness. The mood is emphasised by the alliteration: 'mute and motionless … midnight moments' (10–11).

CHECK THE POEM

A poem by Branwell which explores the nature of death in a more general way, rather than the death of one person, is 'Lines ("We leave our bodies in the Tomb")'. This seems to question the possibility of an afterlife. His 'O God! while I in pleasure's wiles' also echoes 'On Caroline' in its acknowledgement that life's pleasures inevitably end in death.

The day is 'void of sunlight' (12), but most gothic of all is the image of the speaker's 'raven-pinioned dream/ Of coffin, shroud, and sepulchre' (15–16).

In the third stanza the poem employs a popular technique: the speaker asks himself, rhetorically, how he can still be alive when his loved one is dead, even taunting himself with the impossibility of forgetting her, as if he might think for a moment that he could. The final stanza goes one step further, declaring that even joy itself is a mere ghost, since causes of sorrow remain fresh and powerful, while memories of happiness fade away. In calling his loved one 'thy borrowed bride' (32), he implies that life is temporary and happiness only ever conditional. The reality, he would have us believe, is contained in the personification of 'cares' as 'life's conquerors' (27), stronger and more enduring than happiness.

GLOSSARY	
15	pinioned feathered, but also fixed or trapped

'NOW – BUT ONE MOMENT, LET ME STAY'

CONTEXT

At the Battle of Evesham, Simon de Montfort (Earl of Leicester) and the rebel barons were defeated by Prince Edward, later to become King Edward I. Civil war featured often in the Angrian chronicles.

- The speaker savours a moment of calm before joining the Battle of Evesham.

The poem describes a moment of solitary tranquillity in the evening twilight. The narrator allows himself to enjoy an hour of calm before joining the battle whose bugles he can hear in the distance. He describes the sweet stillness, presumably all the sweeter for his knowing that, for him, it cannot last. Finally, and ominously, he describes the faint but pervading sound of the distant battle.

COMMENTARY

Although theoretically narrated by a soldier about to join the Battle of Evesham (4 August 1265), this poem could relate to anyone about to join a battle. It could also relate to the fantasy world of

Angria. More metaphorically speaking, it could describe any situation in which one is briefly able to seize a moment of calm before entering into tumult.

The mood of the poem is very different from that of 'On Caroline'. Here the phrasing subtly creates a sense of the fleeting moment. There is none of the long-drawn-out development of ideas found in the former poem, as if the speaker simply has not time for that. Phrases such as 'Now – but one moment' (1) and 'dash amid the strife' (6) create a sense of urgency: there is no time to waste. On the other hand, the poem is given depth by the speaker seizing what little time he has to contemplate his surroundings. The calm of nature is in contrast with the noise and violence of the distant battle: 'The shade of quiet trees' (12), the 'sweet evening breeze' (14), the empty 'twilight sky' (15), with its 'veil' (like a nun or a modest young woman) of clouds 'All sleeping calm and grey' (16–17).

The soldier sounds familiar with war, judging by his description of it in the second stanza, in which war is personified as 'sullen' (8), the repetition of this word perhaps suggesting the inexorable progress of the battle. The personification is continued in the striking 'deep-mouthed voice of war' (10). A different sound of war appears in line 20: 'the sweet trumpet's solemn wail', sounding sweeter in the distance than in the thick of battle.

The final stanza is evocative. Again, it focuses on sound, a sound all the more ominous for its being scarcely heard: the sound of battle, its strangeness and uncertainty reflecting the battle's uncertain outcome.

CHECK THE POEM

Whereas 'Now – but one moment, let me stay' describes a moment of time, a peaceful pause before plunging into battle, Branwell's poem 'Oh, all our cares' describes a place, a 'little lonely spot ... By all unknown and noticed not' where the speaker is able to find respite from the cares of the world.

QUESTION

How do you interpret the 'strange, uncertain sound' of the final stanza? Is it a combination of battle noises, or perhaps something less physical, such as the spirit of war itself?

DEATH TRIUMPHANT

- The poet hopes that the May Day morning will cheer him up.
- He admits to confusing the past, present and future.

CHECK THE POEM

Branwell also explores the powers of recollection in his poems 'Memory' and 'Thorp Green'. There, however, memory seems to be largely restorative rather than confusing.

This is a somewhat puzzling poem, not least because its title seems to bear little relation to its content. The first stanza is relatively straightforward: the poet expresses a hope that the bright May Day morning will lift his spirits and restore happy memories. He begins the second stanza still addressing the 'Sweet woodland sunshine' (9) and hoping that 'the joys of memory' (10) will bud, like the woodland itself. He seems unwell, and queries the cause of his trembling hand, weary brow and languid limbs. The mood is introspective, bordering on self-pity. He wishes that his body could feign good health, comparing it with his soul, which, aided by 'caprice of fancy' (22), or imagination, is only too good at making the unreal seem real, in particular making him confuse the present, past and future.

COMMENTARY

This is an introspective poem, in which the poet explores his own unhappiness and confusion, as well as the underlying theme of memory. There is, of course, a positive element, in that the occasion of the poem is a bright May Day morning, which the poet hopes will influence his mood. However, a great deal of uncertainty is produced by the unanswered questions – six altogether. In lines 14–18 he is, in essence, asking 'What is the matter with me?' This is rather weakly linked to the remainder of the poem by the wish expressed in lines 19–21 that the 'mortal Self', the body, could be as good at pretending as the soul, which is linked to imagination. He may wish to be cured of his sickness, or of the effects of ageing.

QUESTION

When Branwell asks if he is 'the child of Gambia's side', do you think he is questioning whether he is the same person that he was as a child, or whether he still has access to the happiness he felt then?

In line 24 the iambic metre falters (having one syllable too many for easy scansion), perhaps reflecting the uncertainty that makes the poet unsure whether he has already told a particular story, or makes him imagine that a fantasy future ('A phantom path of joys', 27) can become reality. His introspection deepens, it seems, as he even wonders if he is his own childhood self – Gambia being a river in the fantasy world of Angria that Branwell created as a child with Charlotte. The poem ends on a note of longing, as Branwell contemplates the freedom and happiness of childhood.

GLOSSARY

17	languid	lacking energy
19	dissemble	pretend, feign
22	caprice	whim

TO SESTIUS

- The narrator says that spring has come and encourages Sestius to enjoy it while it lasts: soon the dark night of Death will descend upon us.

The poem's narrator announces the coming of spring. Stanza 1 lists several indications that winter has ended, while the first part of stanza 2 urges Sestius to enjoy spring while he can. As the remainder of the poem warns, death comes, all too soon, to rich and poor, and the dead are beyond the delights of wine and love.

COMMENTARY

This poem is Branwell's translation of an ode by the Roman poet Horace. As such, it is of special interest in terms of the language with which Branwell has attempted to convey Horace's meaning. Branwell's translation of Horace is fairly free, as was necessary to accommodate his new and slightly complex rhyme scheme (*ababbcbcc*) and a change to iambic pentameter. He has chosen to translate *Favoni* (the west wind accompanying spring) as 'the breeze of spring' (1), and he has dropped the mention of *Cytherea*, an island near where Venus (or the Greek Aphrodite) was said to have risen from the sea. On the other hand, his translation expands Horace's original, which consists of only twenty lines. Branwell extends Horace's mention of *imminente Luna* (the moon, Luna, overhead) to 'rising moons each balmy evening' (5). He has added even more new material in his final stanza. The beautiful lines 19–20 are entirely his own, as are the last two lines of the poem, which introduce the wonderful image of Lycidas shining like the sun, eclipsing all others in his 'beams' (27).

 CHECK THE NET

For another translation of the **ode** which Branwell calls 'To Sestius', see *The Odes and Carmen Sæculare of Horace*, translated into English verse by John Conington. The same translation is available online, for example at **http://ancienthistory.about.com**. Search for 'Horace odes', click on 'Odes of Horace in English translation' and then scroll down or search for Book I, Ode IV '*Solvitur Acris Hiems*'.

CONTEXT

The Roman poet now widely known as Horace (Quintus Horatius Flaccus), lived 65–8 BCE, during the reign of Augustus, who befriended him. Horace studied philosophy in Athens and served as a soldier before being acclaimed as a poet.

CHECK THE NET

The original Latin text of Horace's **ode** is available at **www.perseus.tufts.edu**. Search for 'Shorey Horatius', click on 'Q. Horatius Flaccus' and enter 1.4.1 into the search box.

CHECK THE POEM

Another poet who employed the image of death used by Horace as translated in 'To Sestius' (14–15) was William Cowper, who begins his poem 'Stanzas' (1787) with a different translation of these lines: 'Pale death with equal foot strikes wide the door/ Of royal halls and hovels of the poor.'

CHECK THE POEM

John Milton (1608–74) wrote a poem called 'Lycidas', which is an **elegy** to a drowned friend.

In stanza 1, Branwell's translation effectively captures the change of the season. Ships return to sea after being refitted over the winter. Now 'hoar frosts' no longer 'whiten over field and tree' (4). Such phrases as 'balmy evening', 'merry dances tripping' and 'roaring furnace shine' (5–8) all help to create a sense of joyful activity and growing warmth. Branwell's translation of Horace's *Pallida Mors* as 'pallid Death' (14) is literal but effective. The addition at the start of stanza 3 is especially effective as a **metaphor** for death: 'Soon shall the night that knows no morning come' (19). Branwell could perhaps have reworded the awkwardly Latinate lines 22–3: 'Where Thee the well thrown dice may never more/ Make monarch, while thy friends the wine cup pour.' They refer to the fact that a throw of the dice would determine who was the judge, or 'king', in Roman drinking games.

GLOSSARY	
title	Sestius Lucius Sestius, a Roman consul in 23 BCE
6	Venus Roman goddess of love, and more generally of beauty and harmony. She was also the ruler of the astrological sign of Taurus, and thus associated with the period from the end of April to the end of May
	Nymphs nature spirits
	Graces three goddesses associated with joy, beauty and happiness
7	lea meadow
8	Vulcan blacksmith of the Roman gods, associated with fire and iron
9	Cyclops according to the Greek historian Hesiod, three giants who forged Jupiter's thunderbolts, and who were therefore busy in early summer preparing for summer thunderstorms
13	Faunus Roman god who protected cattle, sheep and agriculture
21	Pluto Roman god of death and the underworld
24	Lycidas a beautiful shepherd boy, first described by the Greek poet Theocritus, who was regarded as the ideal of innocent youth

PENMAENMAWR

- The poet describes a craggy hill overlooking the Menai Straits, North Wales, seen from the sea.
- He compares himself with the hill.
- He laments the end of a relationship and wishes for Penmaenmawr's powers of endurance.

Branwell is moved by wild November weather to recall gazing tearfully at the hill of Penmaenmawr while a ship's Scots band played mournfully. He reflects on how he once thought that his will and vigour could overcome obstacles, rather as the ancient fort on the hill has resisted attacks. He envies the imperturbability of Penmaenmawr, which is in contrast to his own grief and desolation. Recalling his lost love, he wishes for Penmaenmawr's 'stony brow' (69), or even a breast of stone, so that he might withstand grief.

COMMENTARY

The poem recollects Branwell's sailing on a steamer through the Menai Straits (between the Welsh mainland of Snowdonia and the island of Anglesey). He sent the poem to his friend J. B. Leland in November 1845, with the following note:

> These lines only have one merit – that of … really expressing my feelings while sailing under the Welsh mountain – When the band on board the steamer struck up 'Ye banks and braes' – and God knows that, for many different reasons, those feelings were far enough from pleasure.
>
> (Quoted in Smith, Margaret (ed.), *The Letters of Charlotte Brontë*, OUP, 2007)

In the poem, Branwell refers to the song here called 'Ye banks and braes', by Robert Burns, as 'Old Scotland's song' (15), slightly misquoting Burns's words as 'times departed, – never to return' (16). This sets the tone for the poem, since Burns's poem is about lost love, and 'Penmaenmawr' was inspired by Branwell's feelings of loss

 CHECK THE NET
See **www. rhylphotosoc. co.uk** for pictures of Penmaenmawr, including the hill or mountain about which Branwell wrote. Go to 'Gallery' and click on 'Penmaenmawr'.

 CHECK THE POEM
Robert Burns's poem 'Ye banks and braes' asks the banks and braes (hillsides) of the Doon Valley in Scotland how they can bloom so fair when he is heartbroken, and complains that the 'warbling bird' reminds him of '…departed joys,/ Departed, never to return'.

CONTEXT

Branwell apparently hoped to marry Lydia Robinson one day. However, his affair with her led to his dismissal by her husband from his post as tutor at Thorp Green, which prevented him from having further contact with her. In an attempt to recover his emotional equilibrium, and now having time on his hands, Branwell went on holiday with his friend John Brown, to Liverpool, from where pleasure steamers set out to cruise along the scenic North Wales coastline.

CHECK THE POEM

An earlier and more hopeful poem in which Branwell compares the restless and changeful nature of the sea with his, or a **narrator's**, emotions is 'Augusta'.

at the enforced ending of his relationship with his employer's wife, Lydia Robinson. The poem is in rhyming couplets of iambic pentameter, also known as heroic couplets. This form, with its end-stopped lines and line-end stresses, creates a feeling of weightiness that matches the subject matter, giving a certain heroic grandeur to Branwell's feelings.

Branwell identifies closely with the 'tempest-beaten form' (2) of Penmaenmawr and the 'restless sea' (5) beneath it, considering his own heart to be similarly 'worn down by care' (10). The mournful echo of the Scottish music from the shore reflects his own sad feelings. Much of the language of the poem suggests restlessness and unease. Branwell compares the 'mighty fort' on Penmaenmawr, which has been 'turned to scattered stones' (24), to his own former youthful confidence, now worn down by 'ceaseless strife and change' (36). However, the poem also contains the Romantic concept of the sublime – that which is noble, majestic and inspiring, particularly in nature (see especially line 4).

In the section of the poem, beginning at line 37, Branwell envies Penmaenmawr's 'better fate'. It has preserved its 'unshaken realm' (48), whereas he is now broken by 'hopeless grief' (55). He mourns his lost hope of love, 'a flower, whose leaves were meant to bloom' (53) and refers to Lydia Robinson's 'tender form' (61), but it is unclear whether the next line ('Beaten, unsheltered, by affliction's storm') refers to her or to himself – perhaps the latter as this would continue his identification with the storm-battered hill of Penmaenmawr. Certainly the line 'An arm – a lip – that trembled to embrace' (63) has to refer to himself, as he is trembling to embrace his lover's 'gentle breast and sorrowing face' (64). And it is Branwell whose mind clings to 'Ouse's fertile side' (65) – the River Ouse ran close to Thorp Green, home of the Robinsons – while he is tossing on the sea.

In the two last stanzas, Branwell addresses his soul, asking if he can develop Penmaenmawr's powers of endurance. Again, he strives for a heroic tone in the reference to Wales being attacked with 'fire and sword' (76) by Edward I of England. He wishes that he could be as unmoved as this craggy hill.

GLOSSARY

3	yon that (with the sense of 'over there')
7	Arvon name given to this part of North Wales
43	verdant grassy, green
52	Mona Welsh name for the isle of Anglesey
55	blanching turning pale

EMILY JANE BRONTË

'TELL ME, TELL ME, SMILING CHILD'

- A speaker questions a child about its life.
- The child answers with references to nature.

This deceptively simple poem is in question and answer form. In the opening of each stanza a speaker asks a child a question, and in the second part of the stanza the child appears to answer. In the first stanza the questioner takes two lines in order to address the 'smiling child', and in the other two stanzas only one. The questions asked relate to the child's perspective on its past, present and future. The child's answers are all in the form of metaphors from the natural world.

COMMENTARY

This poem is actually quite subtle on close inspection. The questioner appears to be an adult, who simply asks questions without commenting on the answers. The 'smiling child' is presumably portrayed as happy because of its simple connection to nature, which to Emily often takes on the role of nurturing mother. The child answers in metaphors rather than attempting an 'adult' analysis of the question. Whereas to adults in Emily's poems time is often a source of sadness, ultimately leading to death and the loss of self, this child knows nothing of death and sees time only in relation to nature, and especially the seasons.

CHECK THE BOOK

Branwell's affair at Thorp Green, followed by his sick-bed ravings and self-pity, probably inspired Anne's portrayal of Huntingdon in *The Tenant of Wildfell Hall*, and some of the intense, romantic scenes in *Wuthering Heights*.

CONTEXT

Emily Brontë's use of childhood innocence as an embodiment of spiritual purity, as found in 'Tell me, tell me, smiling child', is reminiscent of some of the poems in William Blake's *Songs of Innocence* (1789), such as 'Holy Thursday', which describes children as innocent lambs 'with radiance all their own'. It was the **Romantic** poets who introduced the idea of childhood as a time of ideal innocence.

CHECK THE POEM

Emily Brontë also uses the technique of question and answer in 'Come hither, child' and 'To A. G. A.'. She was probably influenced by the traditional ballad form, which sometimes uses the same technique. 'Sir Patrick Spens' (widely available online), for example, uses the same metre. The form was given literary status by **Romantic** poets, especially Wordsworth and Coleridge, whose *Lyrical Ballads* was published in 1798.

The first metaphor describes the past as an autumn evening, combining the idea of the turning year and the fading day in one image. It is 'soft and mild' (4) both in terms of weather, and like a loving mother, perhaps known by the child in infancy and since lost, as hinted at by the wind that 'sighs mournfully' (4). The wind also suggests the dying of the year, and other losses of the past. The alteration of the largely trochaic metre in this line forces us to drag it out limpingly if speaking it aloud.

The second metaphor, describing the 'present hour' (5), most closely relates to the child, appropriately as a child lives largely in the present moment. The branch, with new leaves and blossom on which a young bird sits about to fly away, is like the growing child.

The final metaphor pictures the future as a sunlit sea – the sea being a frequently occurring symbol for infinity in Emily's poems (in 'No Coward Soul is Mine', for example). The image is confident and optimistic, picturing the future as a return of the individual to the undifferentiated whole. The tone here suggests Emily's own desire to escape into that realm.

The rhyme scheme is fairly simple, though a sense of completion is achieved in the final stanza by the change from alternately rhyming lines to rhyming couplets. There seems to be a particular use of rhyme to reinforce meaning in this stanza: the child ('happy *one*') is identified with the 'cloudless sun' and the 'sea' with 'infinity' (9–12). The child, in its innocence, possesses a timeless wisdom.

'ALONE I SAT'

- The poet complains that inspiration has abandoned her.
- She realises that inspiration must come naturally, not through striving.

This is a poem about being abandoned by inspiration. The poet recalls sitting alone on a summer evening and being much moved by the 'solemn joy' (9) of the evening, yet unable to express that feeling in words. Despite having been surrounded by dreams and visions since childhood, she remained uninspired and dispirited.

COMMENTARY

The poem is not quite as paradoxical as it may seem at first, since it expresses, in Wordsworth's words, 'emotion recollected in tranquillity'. In other words, the poet is describing a time in the past when she lacked inspiration, not writing about lacking it in the present moment. Even when she says, in the final stanza, 'But now when I had hoped…' (19), she is referring to what she *said* to herself on this past occasion.

The poet recalls a past summer evening, following on from a day partially personified as 'smiling' (2), then dying. An atmosphere of intimacy and mystery is engendered by the 'misty hill and breezeless glade' (4). This calm, however, is dramatically broken by the change of rhyme and rhythm in stanza 2. The lines become longer and the metre partly anapaestic ('And my heart bowed beneath their power', 6), suggesting surging waves of feeling – a suggestion added to by the use (and rhyming) of the words 'rushing' (5) and 'gushing' (7). The repetition of 'And' at the start of each line also contributes to the sense of mounting pressure. There are even two extra lines in this stanza, and the whole stanza builds to a climax that comes with the rhyming of 'hour' (10) with 'power' (6). As the word 'divine' (10) reveals, she is speaking of a mystical experience.

The third stanza, in which the poet recollects asking herself why heaven has withheld inspiration, seems slightly prosaic after the second. The fourth pictures the poet as a carefree child in her 'sunny … morning prime' (16–18), like the child in 'Tell me, tell me, smiling child', nourished by her passionate imagination. The final stanza is punctuated as a new sentence but actually carries on the sense of the previous one, completing the poet's quotation of what she apparently asked herself at the time of the experience, begun in line 11. It employs a musical metaphor, variations on which are often used for poetic inspiration in poems of this era and earlier: the poet hoped to sing but finds she strikes 'a tuneless string' (20) (as on a

**CHECK
THE BOOK**

Wordsworth's definition of poetry as 'emotion recollected in tranquillity' is included in the 1802 preface to *Lyrical Ballads*. Stanza 2 in 'Alone I sat' is reminiscent of Wordsworth's 'Prelude' (1805), in which he is awed by the 'Presences of Nature, in the sky/ And on the earth! Ye Visions of the hills!/ And Souls of lonely places!' (lines 490–2).

**CHECK
THE POEM**

Another poem in which Emily boldly introduces a new metre to match new subject matter is 'A. E. and R. C.'.

QUESTION

Shelley, in his 'Defence of Poetry' (1819), wrote that it was 'an error to assert that the finest passages of poetry are produced by labour and study'. Does the ending of 'Alone I sat' simply mean that striving to write poetry is pointless, or does it imply that life itself has no purpose?

QUESTION

Snow features in several of Emily Brontë's poems, including 'Song by Julius Brenzaida to G. S.', 'Loud without the wind was roaring', 'Come, walk with me' and 'Remembrance'. Is it possible to identify a shared **symbolism** in the poems' use of snow?

harp). The phrase 'the burden of the strain' (21) has several meanings. In terms of the metaphor it is the chorus or refrain of the song or tune, but it also carries the meanings of heaviness and stress, which lead the poet to end on what could be seen as a note of despair.

GLOSSARY	
17	fancy imagination
21	burden the refrain or chorus of a song
	strain a tune or song

TO A WREATH OF SNOW, BY A. G. ALMEDA

- The speaker, A. G. Almeda, is a prisoner in a dungeon.
- She addresses the snow that comforts her in her captivity.

This poem is notionally spoken by Augusta Geraldine Almeda, the central heroine of the Gondal narrative invented by Emily and Anne. She is being held captive in a dungeon and is comforted to catch a glimpse of snow from her cell. It reminds her of the mountains in her native land. The poem is addressed to the snow, as if it were human.

COMMENTARY

The poem begins with two ode-like lines hailing the snow as if it is a passing ship driven astray by an 'adverse wind' (3) to the speaker's dungeon. The fact that the snow is a 'voyager of heaven' (1) and not 'the *heavens*' shows that it is both snow in the normal sense and, on another level, a divine 'messenger', as it is termed in the final stanza (25). As in some other poems, such as 'The Prisoner', Emily is using imprisonment as a metaphor for the earthbound human condition. The comfort she seeks, and finds in the snow, is spiritual transcendence.

In the second and third stanzas the speaker marvels that her captor, a rebel identified as 'the hands…' that have shut the sun from her 'mourning brow' (5–6), has not been able to prevent the entry of the snow, commenting that he would have done so had he realised what comfort it gave his prisoner – which suggests that he must be very cruel to want to deny her even this comfort.

The poem reaches a low point in stanza 4. The repetition in line 13 emphasises the monotony of the prisoner's existence, and that she has been imprisoned for some time. The 'sinking gloom' (14) refers both to her heart and the darkness of her cell. This depressive effect is heightened by the homophone linking 'morning', which should normally be a relatively cheerful time, with 'mourning'.

In the remaining three stanzas the poem climbs steadily in mood and imagery. The snow is angelic, and it has, for the prisoner, a sweet voice that reminds her of her 'native summits drear'. The fact that she prefers these to 'greenest plains below' (23–4) points to Emily's own pleasure in melancholy dreariness. The last stanza reaches a climax: the snow is not merely comforting, but 'thrilling' (26); there is a sense of ecstasy in the sibilance of 'voiceless, soulless, messenger/ Thy presence…' (25–6). The prisoner anticipates being sustained by this feeling even after the snow has gone. The snow, in essence, represents the divine, which offers the freedom of self-transcendence even within the confines of human existence.

CHECK THE POEM

Shelley's 'Ode to the West Wind' addresses the wind in a similar way to this poem. It begins: 'O Wild West Wind, thou breath of Autumn's being.'

QUESTION

How convincing do you find the passion expressed in this poem?

GLOSSARY

10	talisman comforting good luck charm

F. DE SAMARA TO A. G. A.

- The speaker, F. De Samara, is about to commit suicide for love of A. G. A.
- He stabs himself but even in his dying words he cannot conquer his love.

This is another Gondal poem, in effect Fernando De Samara's suicide note, addressed to Augusta Geraldine Almeda, Queen of Gondal. De Samara is about to die for love of Augusta, with whom he has had a tempestuous relationship. He wishes that she could experience a fraction of the anguish that he feels because of her. Nonetheless, he cannot extinguish his love for her, even though he succeeds in extinguishing his own life.

COMMENTARY

This poem is reminiscent of the kind of bitter and tempestuous passions that animate *Wuthering Heights*. The speaker appears to be in love with Queen Augusta of Gondal, but his love remains completely unrequited. Nor is she merely indifferent to him; the speaker reveals in stanza 2 that she has hated to see his face. In the penultimate stanza he even speculates that if she were to see him dying, she would only 'Smile in careless pride and utter scorn the while!' (40).

The narrator's situation is unenviable. He is 'drear and lone and far away' (2), the repeated conjunctions hammering home his misery. The phrase 'Cold blows on my breast' (3) can be taken in two senses: the cold wind blows on his breast, and he experiences the violence of 'cold blows' on his breast. The wind, naturally, blows from the north. De Samara's repeated appeal to Augusta to light up her halls, and not to think of him, and for her eyes to remain 'undimmed in their dazzling' (7) shine, betrays a rather self-pitying irony. In effect he is saying 'Don't worry about me – I'll just die here in dreary bleakness while you light up your palace halls for a pleasant evening!'

Although the speaker is on the verge of death, the rhythm of the poem is strong, to match his passion – a fairly regular iambic hexameter. However, many lines are broken by a caesura perhaps hinting either at the rift between the speaker and his beloved, or at his impending break with life. One example is 'The desert moor is dark; there is tempest in the air' (9); in this line the alliteration of 'desert' and 'dark' add to the sense of gloom.

 **QUESTION**

One example of the caesura is 'Do I not see thee now? Thy black resplendent hair'. Can you find others?

The nature of De Samara's 'one last, one burning prayer' (10) is unclear. It may simply be that he will die before dawn. If he is to die by his own hand, which seems to be the case, it was hardly necessary to utter a prayer, unless it were for the resolution to carry out the deed. Even this prayer shows the ambivalence that is a feature of the poem: it sets fire to his heart but freezes on his tongue. This is also an example of the opposites that feature in the poem: fire and ice, hot and cold (lines 3, 10, 12, 33, 42), and light and dark (lines 1, 5, 14, 17, 20, 24, 29). Moreover, he will die, while she will live. Perhaps at a higher level the poem is not merely about two estranged lovers, but about the cosmic battle of opposites that generates the energy of the universe. A similar interpretation could be placed on *Wuthering Heights*, in which Cathy and Heathcliff embody male and female energy, on both a human and a universal level. These lovers are inextricably linked and their feelings for each other combine yearning with destructiveness.

In stanza 4 De Samara sets himself the task of viewing Augusta's likeness (perhaps in a cameo) before he dies. She seems a striking woman: her 'black resplendent hair' and 'glory-beaming brow', her 'smile how heavenly fair' (15–16). Nonetheless, her eyes, in 'Their dark, their deadly ray' (20), seem to be those of a basilisk or of Medusa, creatures who, in ancient myth, could kill with a glance. The repetition of 'their' adds weight to this impression. When he says in the next stanza 'There, go, Deceiver, go! my hand is streaming wet' (21), he appears to be addressing Augusta, although the line is synchronised with his stabbing himself, so he may identify her with the dagger. His hand is wet with his own blood, mentioned in the next line.

It is notable, and perhaps typical of Emily, that in stanzas 6 and 7 De Samara wishes that he could cause his lover pain. Again we think of the ambivalent and far from benign passions of Heathcliff and Cathy in *Wuthering Heights*. To know that Augusta was suffering might enable De Samara to endure his own, otherwise unendurable, anguish (28).

There is a decline in the mood of the poem, if that is possible, in stanza 8: 'How gloomy grows the Night!' (29). De Samara now

CHECK THE POEM

In 'F. De Samara to A. G. A.' the wild weather and bleak surroundings reflect the narrator's feelings, but in 'Song by Julius Brenzaida to G. S.', another of Emily's Gondal poems, they are used to accentuate the intimacy and warmth of the two lovers' feelings, proof against the elements.

CHECK THE POEM

Emily's 'Song: King Julius left the south country' is another poem which embodies the typical high drama of the Gondal poems. However, it is more extrovert than some, describing a doomed military campaign and Julius's subsequent demise. It was probably influenced by 'The Destruction of Sennacherib', by Lord Byron (1788–1824), a poet read by the Brontës.

feels the wind from Gondal, the imaginary land ruled by Augusta, blowing towards him. Whereas in 'To A Wreath of Snow, by A. G. Almeda', the snow takes on the role of messenger, here it is the wind. De Samara exhorts this wind to deliver a message to Augusta, telling her of his 'dreary doom' (35) and warning her of her suffering to come.

In the penultimate stanza, De Samara seems to realise the futility of his own words, and he imagines that Augusta would smile to see his demise. His only satisfaction, in the final stanza, is that although she is the tyrannical ruler of his heart, his love is stronger than her hatred. He may take his life, but his passionate love lives on.

GLOSSARY

9	desert **deserted**

'LOUD WITHOUT THE WIND WAS ROARING'

- On a stormy November day the poet hears a cheering song of spring.
- Her spirits are lifted and she recalls youthful expeditions to the moors near her home.
- She is brought back to stark reality by the sight of the heath.

Written while Emily was away from home, teaching at Law Hill, this poem is essentially about her homesickness and her attempts to combat it. At the same time, it relates to wider feelings of despondency – perhaps to what one could call 'divine homesickness', a longing for a lost spiritual realm. It is November and the weather is stormy, but her spirits are temporarily lifted by hearing a song about spring. She is moved by the second line of the song to recall rising at dawn and going out to enjoy the moors, perhaps with Charlotte and Anne. Then, however, she is brought back to a realisation of the grim present by the sight of the 'brown heath' (54).

COMMENTARY

As often in Emily's poems, the weather – and especially wild or dismal weather – sets the scene. The first line crashes into being with the rolling 'Loud without the wind was roaring', the placing of the word 'Loud' at the start of the line emphasising the volume. The poet's mood matches the weather of 'that dreary eve' (5) until the words of an ancient song come to her, reminding her of spring. The first line of the song is quoted as line 11: 'It was spring, for the skylark was singing'. The words lift her spirits, despite the absence of friends and her distance from home (14). She seems to summon the moorland wind, asking it to call her 'To walk by the hill-river's side!' (22). We feel Emily's passion for the moors in these lines. Strangely, she imagines the stream in winter, not in spring, when there are no 'yellow-stars' or 'blue-bells' (30). For her, the winter moors of her youth are lovelier and more evocative than summer cornfields.

A second line of the uplifting spring song is injected into the poem at line 35, reminding her of the time when she and her sisters rose 'blithely' (39) at dawn. The 'amber and blue' (40) of the sky makes the memory spring to life, and we feel Emily's huge enthusiasm in the repeated 'For the moors' (43–7), uttered five times like the chorus of a song. We hear, with her, the exuberant song of the linnet and skylark, until – just at the point of her spirit rising with the skylark – she is dashed down by the 'brown heath' (54) reminding her of the reality of her 'exile afar' (52) , both exile from home (at Law Hill) and from heaven as a human being living on earth. The very heath whispers to her of its imprisonment by 'grim walls' (57), echoing her own feelings.

The poem becomes confused at this point. The 'loved music whose waking/ Makes the soul of the Swiss die away'(59–60) is the mountain wind: we are asked to believe that the love of the Swiss for this wind is so great as to send them into a swoon. However, the confusion comes about because the 'brown heath' that depressed the poet in lines 55–8 now has a 'spell more adored and heart-breaking', in the 'half-blighted bells' (61–2) of its heather, than the mountain wind supposedly has for the Swiss. The reason for this

**CHECK
THE POEM**

The wild highland landscape of many of Emily's poems is inspired as much by the Scottish Highland settings of the novels of Sir Walter Scott (1731–1832) as by the moors of her native Haworth. A particularly telltale poem in this respect is 'Song: The linnet in the rocky dells', which describes 'wild deer' browsing, more a feature of the Highlands than of Haworth. Scott's most famous novels include *The Heart of Midlothian* (1818) and *Ivanhoe* (1819).

CHECK THE POEM

Emily's delight in the varied faces of nature is found in many of her poems, for example in the lively 'Will the day be bright or cloudy?', which is based on the idea that a firstborn girl child's future can be predicted by the weather on the day of her birth.

seems to be that this heath both reminds her sweetly of home yet saddens her when she recalls how far away from home she is.

In the penultimate stanza, Emily speaks of her spirit burning to be free. Finally, she consoles herself with the thought that time, however laden with troubles, is passing, and that she will eventually be reunited with her siblings.

GLOSSARY	
24	hoar covered with ice crystals
27	yellow-stars may refer to the flower tormentil, a flower in a cross shape, named for Christ's torment on the Cross, or to the celandine

'THE BLUE BELL IS THE SWEETEST FLOWER'

- The poet speaks of the bluebell's power to console.
- She mourns its absence in winter.

Like so many of Emily's poems, this one takes as its theme the power of nature to console or inspire her and to stir her memories. Like 'Loud without the wind was roaring', with which it is grouped in her notebook, this poem's setting is winter. The poet describes the winter landscape and expresses her longing for spring and for the consoling power of the bluebell, and for her home.

COMMENTARY

The poem is set in winter, a time whose bleakness so often accords with Emily's own mood. She wrote it shortly before Christmas, when away from home teaching at Law Hill. The subject of the poem is fairly simple, as is the more or less regular iambic metre and *abab* rhyme scheme. The poet commences with a comment on the bluebell's power to soothe her spirit. She acknowledges the 'spell in purple heath' (the heather) and the fragrance of the violet (5, 7) but implies that neither of these can compare with the bluebell. She describes the cold ('ice', 'frozen mist') and dark ('sombre shade') of winter (stanza 4) and mourns the absence of the bluebell, the violet and the heather flowers. However, it is to the bluebell that she returns, painting a vivid picture of its paradoxically 'slight and stately stem' (29) and its bright colours, appropriately jewel-like because of the flower's preciousness to her. As is often the case with Emily, the memory of the bluebell arouses mixed feelings. It soothes her but brings tears to her eyes because of the absence of the actual flower.

Although much of this poem is fairly commonplace, the last two verses rise above the rest. The poet pictures winter sunlight falling 'Adown the dreary sky' (42) and gilding the 'dank and darkened wall/ With transient brilliancy' (43–4), the heavy **alliteration** contrasting with the image of fleeting gleams of light. This makes her yearn for 'the time of flowers to come' and to miss 'the fields of home' (46–8). As is often the case, absent or fading nature triggers the homesickness that to Emily is almost innate. Moreover, it suggests a more general sense of mortality.

'COME HITHER, CHILD'

- A lady reprimands a child harpist for rousing her emotions.
- The child tells how she heard the tune long ago, in a kind of mystical visitation.

This rather mysterious poem relates to a lost Gondal narrative. A child is playing a stringed instrument, probably a harp, to a lady, perhaps Queen Augusta of Gondal. The lady demands to know how the child learned to play so well and how she dares to stir the lady to thoughts that she would rather not entertain. The child explains how she sought solitude one night and in the depths of private misery was visited by mysterious music.

 CHECK THE POEM

The child's tale in 'Come hither, child' is reminiscent of the knight's tale in Keats's *La Belle Dame Sans Merci*, which also has a medieval setting, popular in **gothic** poetry.

CHECK THE POEM

Emily's 'The Prisoner' is a fully **framed narrative**, beginning and ending with the same male narrator. The female prisoner's narrative is framed (contained) within his.

CHECK THE NET

The otherworldly power of the harp in 'Come hither, child' may be compared with stories of the Irish mythological god the Dagda, who was said to possess a magical harp on which he played the Three Noble Strains of Ireland. Go to **www.livingmyths. com** and search for 'Dagda'.

COMMENTARY

This poem would perhaps be more satisfying if it began and ended with the voice of the lady. As it is, her rather imperious questions, the second more rhetorical than the first, take up the first stanza but have no conclusion. Evidently she is moved by the child's music to thoughts and emotions that she would rather forget.

The child, apologising for awakening these feelings, tells a strange story. She says she first heard the tune in 'Ula's hall' (7), Ula being a province of Gaaldine in the Gondal sagas. Her tale is gothic in character. She abandons the 'crowds and light' (11) of a party to seek somewhere dark and cold (one wonders why), perhaps to match her lonely mood. In the 'lonely room' (19) she imagines a host of fearful forms, as if the room is haunted, and prays in her misery that she might die. But, as if in answer to her prayer, she hears instead a note 'so deeply sweet' (26) that she thinks it is Judgement Day and the Angel Gabriel has come to take her to heaven.

As if in a fairytale, the music sounds three times. It is angelic, a 'seraph-strain' (29). It is unclear whether what she hears is literally a note, or whether, as is more likely, this stands for a tune, which has haunted her ever since and which she has played to the lady in stanza 1.

We have in this poem the familiar features of dark, cold, loneliness, sorrow, 'silence drear' (23) lit up, albeit temporarily, by a seemingly divine visitation, like the snow in 'To A Wreath of Snow, by A. G. Almeda'. The poem is striking, mysterious, yet frustratingly inconclusive. Its dark mood is gothic, but its portrayal of the apparently abandoned child, along with the triple sounding of the angelic note, is reminiscent of fairytales. Cinderella, for example, is similarly lonely and unloved.

GLOSSARY		
5	chide	reprimand
9	festal	festival or celebratory
		continued

27	Gabriel angel expected to sound a trumpet to signal Judgement Day (the end of the world)
29	seraph an angel of the first order, normally pictured as a child's winged head

QUESTION

The child in 'Come hither, child' seems comfortless. How far do you think Emily may have been drawing on her own childhood in writing this poem?

SONG ('O BETWEEN DISTRESS AND PLEASURE')

- The narrator declines to settle for mere friendship after a passionate relationship has ended.
- He determines to go away, leaving the loved one in peace.
- He foresees a time when his lover has completely forgotten him.

CHECK THE POEM

Many poets have addressed poems to their lover on their final separation. One of the best is the sonnet 'Since there's no help, come, let us kiss and part' by Michael Drayton (1563–1631).

This pithily passionate poem seems to be narrated by a male persona (given the determination to become 'an Ocean rover', 12), who has been rejected by a lover. He says that love, 'Fond affection' (2), cannot survive somewhere 'between distress and pleasure' (1). In other words, love must have all or nothing. Only 'Wretched hearts' (3) would accept mere friendship.

With bitter realism, the narrator explains why friendship is not possible: his lover would never smile while he was still grieving – so could never be carefree in his company, yet he could hardly expect her to be sympathetic to him for ever. Resolutely, he proclaims that it is time to part, and that once he has gone she will sleep more peacefully and never have to feign sorrow when she sees him. She will in time completely forget him.

COMMENTARY

This poem has a wonderful vigour. The sturdy trochaic metre, with second and fourth lines in each stanza each falling one syllable short of the eight syllables found in the first and third lines, gives an impression of noble resolution. The regular *abab* rhyme scheme is made more expansively eloquent by the effective use of

CHECK THE POEM

A more modern poem in which a lover contemplates the links between himself and his partner gradually fading is Philip Larkin's 'No Road' (*Collected Poems*). He imagines the connection between them as a road, subject to 'all time's eroding agents'.

enjambment, especially between the third and fourth lines, as in '...treasure/ Friendship's joys when others flee' (3–4). The sense continues smoothly from one line to the next despite the rhyme, contrasting with other end-stopped lines, such as 'Lands where woe may wander free' (14). Thus there is a contrast between ending and continuation, which matches the way in which the relationship ends but life goes on. Alliteration, as in line 14, or in lines 19–20, also adds to a sense of vigour and resilience in the face of loss.

The forsaken lover of this poem strikes a rather romantic pose, declaring:

> I will be an Ocean rover,
> I will sail the desert sea. (12–13)

The repetition of 'I will' is determined. He could almost add, 'I will survive!' He seems careless of his fate in his sweeping suggestion that he will banish himself to 'Lands where woe may wander free' (14), identifying himself casually with woe itself. At the same time, there may be an intentional irony in his assurance that his lover's pillow will be all the softer for his absence, or his desire to save her from having to feign sorrow on his behalf.

The ending of the poem deliciously blends bitter cynicism (the dismissive 'some dreary token', 21) with the poignancy of real loss: 'I shall be a dream to thee' (24). This last line leaves us with the feeling that the narrator's bravado does indeed conceal a broken heart.

GLOSSARY	
12	**desert** deserted
21	**token** an image of the past that reawakens memories

'LOVE IS LIKE THE WILD ROSE BRIAR'

- The poet compares love and friendship through the **similes** of a wild rose and a holly tree.

This simple poem makes a comparison between love, the wild rose briar, and friendship, the holly tree, using rhetorical questions to make a moralistic point. It expresses a preference for friendship as being more lasting than love.

COMMENTARY

Like many of Emily's poems, this one features the seasonal round, and suggests that winter will be the true test of the individual's resilience. The poem has the ring of bitter experience, even though, as far as we know, Emily had no first-hand experience of love. The rather platitudinous tone is at odds with the way in which Emily presents love in *Wuthering Heights*, in which love is not a 'silly rose-wreath' (9) but a monumental, all-consuming passion.

The first stanza makes the comparison; the second appeals to the senses, bringing to mind the fragrance of the rose in spring and summer. The final stanza supplies the moral: if one scorns love in favour of friendship, one will still be happy in old age ('when December blights thy brow', 11).

THE NIGHT-WIND

- The poet sits alone on a summer night.
- The wind tries to seduce her but she resists.

This is one of a number of poems Emily wrote involving a dialogue with nature, here represented by a gentle wind at midnight. The poet tells how one warm summer moonlit midnight as she sat before an open window, she felt the wind speak to her. It is a happy

 QUESTION

Why do you suppose Emily wrote 'Love is like the wild rose briar'? Do you feel that it expresses her real views? Might it have been written to console her sisters, both of whom longed for love?

 QUESTION

How significant is the **personification** of December as a male figure who may 'leave thy garland green'?

 CHECK THE POEM

Compare this poem with Robert Burns's 'Red, red rose' (1792), which begins 'O my Luve's like a red, red rose/ That's newly sprung in June.'

visitation, the wind telling her what she is already feeling – that all is right with the world. However, the wind attempts to seduce her into entering the woods. She resists, and the poem ends with the wind still trying to persuade her.

COMMENTARY

This is a sensuous and mysterious poem, unusual in that the night-wind is given a voice – and a very seductive one at that. The mood of the poem is already sensuously magical before the appearance of the wind. The opening line's alliteration establishes this, and the 'cloudless moon' (2) and dewy rose trees add to this mood. The wind is described in intimate terms, like a lover: 'The soft wind waved my hair' (6); 'its breathing' (9); 'my murmur' (13). This becomes more explicit as the poem goes on: 'Thy wooing voice is kind' (18); 'Its kiss grew warmer still' (26). When the wind refuses to take no for an answer, sighs sweetly and insists 'O come ... I'll win thee 'gainst thy will' (27–8), the tone is even more that of a persistent wooer seeking to overcome an unconvincing resistance. The wind appeals to their long friendship and finally, in a characteristic reference to death, suggests that life is too short to waste it in this resistance: she will have plenty of time to be alone in the grave, and the wind to mourn her. The suggestion of intimacy is striking, but the anticipation of her death is almost sinister.

The wind's attempt at persuasion is eloquent. The wood at night sounds enchanting: the leaves rustling as if in a dream, and each leaf having a voice 'Instinct (filled with) spirit' (16), in other words, expressing the spirit of nature. There is also a sensuality in the 'scented flower' and 'young tree's supple bough' (21–2) (like human limbs). One wonders why Emily, such a lover of nature, rejects the wind's overtures, preferring her 'human feelings' (23) to run in their own course, like a stream. The sensuality of the language, with its pairings, such as 'murmur ... myriad' (13–15) and 'Wanderer ... warmer' (25–6), suggest that she is tempted. Perhaps it is that, although she is far from being an orthodox Christian, she still sees nature as somehow lower in its sensual appeal than the spiritual heights to which she herself aspires. Perhaps there is even some element of sexual temptation present in the poem.

CHECK THE POEM
Another poem by Emily Brontë in which the wind is given a spiritual presence is 'Aye there it is! It wakes tonight' (*The Brontë Sisters, Selected Poems*, ed. Stevie Davies, Carcanet, 1999).

CHECK THE POEM
The ending of 'The Night-Wind' seems to suggest the same kind of warning found in 'To His Coy Mistress' by Andrew Marvell (1621–78). This warns: 'The grave's a fine and private place,/ But none I think do there embrace.'

It is interesting that in most stanzas only the second and fourth lines rhyme. This makes for a more subtle and persuasive poem than if it had been fully rhyming. It may also suggest a two-way pull: the wind seeks the union implied by rhyme, while the poet's resistance is suggested by the non-rhyming lines.

TO IMAGINATION

- The poet addresses Imagination, **personifying** it as a companion.
- She expresses her gratitude for the blessings of imagination, and contrasts it with the hardships of reality.

In this poem, as in 'Alone I sat', Emily explores the creative process itself. However, whereas in 'Alone I sat' inspiration has failed her, in 'To Imagination' she thanks her imagination for being a kind friend to her. She compares the grim and disheartening world of external reality with the happy internal world of her imagination. Reason and Truth, she says, may pour cold water over the suffering heart's dreams, but imagination is always available to remind the sufferer to hope for better things, even if in itself it is not a substitute for reality.

COMMENTARY

This is a soundly structured poem. Its regular iambic metre reflects the confident and positive tenor. The six-line stanzas are long enough to contain one well-developed main idea in each, the rhyming couplets at the end of each stanza serving to round off the idea. The overall format, however, is not entirely original, being reminiscent of Victorian hymns in which a speaker expresses gratitude that in times of trouble or sadness Jesus is always there to offer comfort. In the case of this poem, the comfort is not Christian but that of the poet's own imagination. She paints a picture of a world of hopeless suffering. She is 'weary with the long day's care/ And earthly change from pain to pain,/ … lost and ready to despair (1–3). Her external world is 'So hopeless', so full of the abstract

---

> **CONTEXT**
>
> **Personification** was much more widely used among nineteenth-century poets than modern ones. A typical example is Wordsworth's 'Ode to Duty'. All the Brontës used personification in their poetry, and Emily uses it to particular effect in 'Imagination' and 'Hope'.

**CHECK
THE POEM**
The **Romantic**
poets, including
Shelley, Keats and
Byron, regarded
imagination highly,
and all four Brontë
siblings wrote
poems about
imagination. See
Charlotte's
'Retrospection',
Branwell's 'Oh, all
our cares', and
Anne's 'Dreams'.

threats of 'guile, and hate, and doubt,/ And cold suspicion' (9–10), not to mention 'Danger, and guilt, and darkness' (14), that she values the 'bright, untroubled sky' (16) all the more. The list of threats, separated by both commas and conjunctions for emphasis, seems overwhelming. Significantly, whereas they are presented as abstract nouns, imagination is characterised in a vivid extended metaphor of 'untroubled sky' filled with 'suns that know no winter days' (16–18). The poet seems to feel at the mercy of external reality, yet is empowered and liberated by her imagination. Her inner world is ruled by a triumvirate: 'thou [Imagination], and I, and Liberty' (11). One is reminded of other poems in which imagination frees the individual from imprisonment, such as 'To a Wreath of Snow, by A. G. Almeda'.

The poem could, in theory, end with the third stanza, Imagination having been thanked and celebrated. However, the poet introduces a further level of sophistication after this point. She has already personified Imagination, and now she personifies Reason, Nature, Truth and Fancy. Whereas Imagination is a kindly friend, Reason dismisses the sufferer's 'cherished dreams' (22). In this preference for imagination over reason, we see Emily as a true child of the Romantics, in the tradition of Keats and Shelley. It is, however, a little more surprising to see Truth personified as behaving so 'rudely' (23) in trampling down the emerging blossoms of Fancy.

For poets of this era, imagination and 'fancy' were generally synonymous, but Emily must make a distinction between the two, since in line 25 she describes how, when Truth has trampled Fancy, Imagination comes to the rescue. It seems that in speaking of Fancy she has in mind something transient and speculative, as in the phrase 'flights of fancy', appropriately represented by flowers. Imagination, on the other hand, seems to refer to the deeper wellspring of creativity that underlies her poetic inspiration. Whereas 'fancy' might be escapist, poetic imagination is not, because it leads to creativity. She knows that in a sense imagination is unreal, 'phantom bliss' (31), but even though she knows the difference between imagination and material reality, ('I trust not ...', 31), it is still a precious solace in times of despair.

GLOSSARY

| 23 | rudely roughly |
| 34 | Benignant benevolent |

REMEMBRANCE

- A woman laments the death of her lover.
- She describes how she learned to live without him.

In this lament, widely regarded as one the best poems in the English language, Emily writes in the persona of a woman addressing her long-dead lover. We should not therefore make the mistake of assuming that Emily is in any direct sense speaking for herself. The speaker begins by incredulously asking herself if it is possible that she has begun to forget her dead lover. She then asks forgiveness for not thinking of him constantly, even though no one has taken his place. Finally, she tells how she made herself quell her emotion, and even turn away from her memories, in order to carry on living.

COMMENTARY

The critic F. R. Leavis wrote in a 1952 article that this poem was insincere, in that it indulged in emotional rhetoric, purporting to express feelings that Emily herself had not felt and could not fully imagine. But the speaker does not indulge her emotions; rather, she reveals how she has learned to deny them in order to survive. The strong rhythms and structure of the poem not only reflect the speaker's stoicism, but also express a powerful emotion which is no less authentic even though Emily had not had this precise experience herself. After all, she had experienced grief and longing, not least relating to the death of her own mother.

In *Wuthering Heights*, and in many nineteenth-century poems, 'recollection' is portrayed as being conscious and usually comforting; 'remembrance', on the other hand, is involuntary. The

 CHECK THE POEM

In 'Remembrance', the **narrator** speaks of suppressing a 'burning wish to hasten/ Down to that tomb already more than mine'. In 'Stanzas' ('I'll not weep that thou art going to leave me', the speaker addresses a dying lover and anticipates her soul 'sighing,/ To go and rest with thee'. 'Remembrance' reads as if it were narrated by the same persona, fifteen years on.

CONTEXT

Some editions give 'Remembrance' its original title: 'R. Alcona to J. Brenzaida', referring to a lost Gondal **narrative** in which Rosina Alcona laments the death of her lover Julius Brenzaida.

? QUESTION

Do you think there could be any significance in the number fifteen in 'Fifteen wild Decembers...' in 'Remembrance'?

repeated phrases in the poem reflect the compulsive nature of emotionally laden memory: 'Cold in the earth' (1, 9), 'Far, far... cold' (2), 'dare not' (29–30). At the same time, the poem moves forward by paradoxes in which remembering is weighed against forgetting. The speaker first asks herself if she has forgotten her lover. If she has begun to do so, she is indeed 'Severed at last by Time's all-severing wave' (4) from him in a way that she was not, so long as she continued to remember him constantly. An earlier manuscript version of the poem has the phrase 'all-wearing wave', suggesting a more gradual process in which memory is eroded by the passage of time. She adds that only the extremely faithful would continue to remember after fifteen years of 'change and suffering' (12), though we cannot be sure whether she includes herself among the faithful few. The language may be rhetorical, meaning that no one can continue to mourn unabated for fifteen years. The constancy she speaks of is contrasted with seasonal change. In addition, the snow of the first stanza has 'melted into spring' (10).

In stanza 4, the speaker asks for forgiveness for not thinking constantly of her lover, and she even speaks of harbouring 'other hopes' (15). However, this is almost contradicted in the next stanza. No one has taken his place, and, even now, all her happiness lies buried with him. Then in stanzas 6 and 7 she explains how she could carry on living, even 'cherishing' her 'existence' (23) (significantly, she avoids the word 'life'). She 'Sternly denied' (27) her despairing, suicidal urges, tearing herself from her lover like a baby from the breast ('Weaned my young soul...', 26). The last stanza reveals the final paradox, appropriately in two strong oxymorons: 'rapturous pain' and 'divinest anguish' (30–1). She dare not allow herself to remember, because in truth such intensely emotional memories would prevent her from continuing in the day to day 'empty world' (32).

CHECK THE POEM

A less complex but similarly passionate poem addressed to an absent (perhaps dead) lover is Emily's 'If grief for grief can touch thee', which has close parallels with Anne's 'Appeal', written shortly afterwards and perhaps, therefore, influenced by Emily's poem.

The development of the poem's thought is matched by a stylistic progression. The poem begins with a powerful two-line exclamation, establishing the elegiac mood, followed by a question establishing the theme. The first statement in the conventional sense is in stanza 2. In the first four stanzas a strong rhythmic feature is the caesura coming midline, like a voice breaking in grief, or as if the line is severed like the two lovers. In stanza 5, a new technique takes over: the powerful repetition in the paired lines. Thereafter the lines are in pairs of opposites: 'golden dreams' give way to 'existence ... cherished ... without the aid of joy' (21–4); 'useless passion' is replaced by stern denial (25–7); and the assertion that she 'Dare not indulge' is contrasted with the savoured thought of 'drinking deep' (30–2), the contrast being enhanced by alliteration.

The overall effect is enhanced by imagery. The cold earth and deep snow have an instantly chilling effect on the senses, which is increased by the dragging dactylic rhythm. The speaker's thoughts, in contrast, are pictured as birds hovering over the mountains. Her lover's burial place is 'on that northern shore' (6), the water here suggesting a barrier between life and death, as well as depth of emotion as in lines 4 and 14.

DEATH

- The poet accuses Death of striking when she least expected it, and commands it to strike again.
- She reflects on the ability of hope and joy to survive human suffering.
- She returns to her desire to die, this time expressing the belief that her death will nourish other life.

The poem, in a sense, is a framed narrative. It begins with a demand that Death should strike again; the next five stanzas express a faith in life and in nature's restorative powers; in the last two stanzas, the poet returns to accusing Death and demanding that she should be struck down so that other lives may flourish. There is perhaps even a sense in which she is asking Death to strike down Time itself so that Eternity may take its place.

COMMENTARY

Commentators are divided as to whether this poem is part of Emily's Gondal narrative, although she wrote it into her non-

> **CONTEXT**
>
> 'Death' relates to two school essays assigned to both Charlotte and Emily: 'The Palace of Death' and 'The Butterfly'. Charlotte uses the former as an opportunity to moralise, linking Intemperance to Nature. Emily associates Intemperance with Civilisation, which will vanquish Death's other servants, including Ambition, Wrath, Fanaticism and Famine. In the second essay, Charlotte takes the metamorphosis of caterpillar into butterfly as a Christian **metaphor** of salvation; in Emily's essay, the caterpillar dies violently so that the butterfly can appear.

Gondal notebook and it contains no references to Gondal characters. On the other hand, at the time of writing Emily had not suffered any recent bereavement, although she had lost her mother at the age of three. It may be then, as some commentators have suggested, that the sudden striking of Death described in stanza 1 refers to Emily becoming aware, at some point in her development, of the reality of death and the inevitability of her own. In other words, her 'certain faith of joy to be' (2) has been shaken into the 'anguish' (27) of the penultimate stanza. The meaning here may be deliberately ambiguous, referring both to coming joy and the joy of being. If this interpretation is correct, then this is a poem about the human condition, since knowledge of personal extinction is something that separates human beings from the animal world. This knowledge, a great cause of 'Sorrow' (10), is related theologically to 'Guilt' (11) and 'Sin' (22).

In this framed narrative, the poet identifies with Time, picturing herself, and time, as a 'withered branch' (3) which springs from Eternity. The divine source of her being is 'fresh' (4), while she, as a human being, is inevitably 'withered'. It is her wish, to which she returns in the final stanza, to return to the perfection of Eternity. In the intervening stanzas, however, the metaphor of herself as 'Time's branch' (5) is developed in a largely positive way. We find water, in the form of 'sap' and 'silver dew' (6) used as a symbol of life and energy. The branch is healthy; it shelters birds and in turn is pollinated by 'wild bees' (8). The ordinary sorrows of human existence 'plucked the golden blossom' of her happiness and 'Guilt' humbled her (9–10), but Mother Nature's 'kindly bosom' (11) restored her.

In stanza 4 we see the poet undaunted, sustained by the comforting words of a personified Hope, and in stanza 5 she describes experiencing a renaissance of joy, a 'second May' (20), alliteratively expressed as a 'beauty-burdened spray' (18) and nurtured by three of the four elements: 'Wind and rain and fervent heat, caressing' (19). This central part of the poem reaches a glorious climax in stanza 6. Her joy is immune to grief, too bright for Sin, and sustained by Love. Only the knowledge of Death (possibly related to the element of earth, as in 'Remembrance') can threaten it. And it

CONTEXT

In her use of the image of the branch in 'Death', Emily Brontë may have been thinking of St John's image of Christ as a vine: 'If a man abide not in me, he is cast forth and withered' (John 15:5).

is this knowledge that strikes in the penultimate stanza. For a moment, the contest hangs in the balance as the poet thinks that 'Evening's gentle air may still restore' (26), but then she dismisses that thought as unrealistic.

The energetic iambic pentameter, with the regular alternation of feminine (last syllable unstressed) and masculine (last syllable stressed) line endings, aptly expresses the poet's determined confrontation of death in the opening and end of the poem, and her energetic embracing of life in the central part. Its regularity of metre could also be seen as expressing the unavoidability of death, as if the poet is bound on the wheel of Time, which is to be condemned to inevitable death.

> **GLOSSARY**
>
> 1   confiding confident

STARS

- The poet regrets the disappearance of the stars with dawn, and with them her sense of oneness with the infinite.
- She longs for the return of night.

This poem, an aubade, is one of the poems in which Emily regrets the passing of a visionary state in which she has experienced a sense of oneness with the infinite. (Another poem containing this theme is 'The Prisoner'.) She associates this state with night, and therefore with the stars, and daytime with the demands of the world which put an end to this state, returning her to alienation from the divine. She sees night as a nurturing mother, and day as an ultimately destructive male figure – although she expresses some ambivalence about this. She does her best to prolong night, and therefore her vision of unity, but has to relinquish it. She ends by praying for the return of night to hide her from the hostile light of day.

> **CONTEXT**
>
> One **aubade** which Emily would certainly have read is the exchange between the two lovers in *Romeo and Juliet* (III. 5. 1–36) in which Juliet protests that it cannot possibly be dawn yet, and that the birdsong they hear must be the nightingale, not the lark. A more modern one is Philip Larkin's last published poem, 'Aubade', in which he anticipates the departure not of a lover, but of his own life.

COMMENTARY

The aubade is a poetic form dating back to the Middle Ages, in which a lover regrets the passing of night because it brings separation from the beloved. In this poem, the place of the beloved is taken by the stars, and by the all-nurturing infinite with which Emily feels she has been in communion. The poem is remarkable in that we view the infinite from the intimacy of the poet's bedroom.

The poem tells a brief narrative, beginning with an accusing question. The poet can hardly believe that the stars have abandoned her, or that her vision of oneness has left her just because the sun has risen. The sky is now 'desert' (4), empty, chiming with her own sense of having been deserted. The poet's description of the 'glorious eyes' (5) that are the stars gazing down at her in a 'watch divine' (8), guarding and sustaining her, is very much a description of the infant's relationship with its mother (as in 'Remembrance'), and the phrase 'drank your beams' (9) suggests suckling. The image of the petrel (12) expands this idea: the seabird is supported by the sea, itself a metaphor for the infinite, as in 'Tell me, tell me, smiling child'. During this blissful night, her thoughts have been like stars dwelling in 'boundless regions' (14), in contrast to the sense of imprisonment in the individual self that Emily so often expresses, and which in this poem is symbolised by the flies imprisoned in her room in stanza 10. The 'one sweet influence' (15) that she has felt is very Wordsworthian, both in its concept and its expression.

Whereas the night has been maternal and sustaining, the sun is pictured as masculine and violent. It is 'dazzling' (1), it scorches 'with fire' (19), its 'blood-red' colour and 'arrow-straight ... fierce beams' speak of murder, and strike her brow fiercely (21–3). The poet seeks shelter from its 'hostile light,/ That does not warm, but burn' (43–4). The sun invades her privacy even through the veil of her eyelids (25). Moreover, whereas she addressed the stars intimately in the second person, as 'you', she holds the sun at arm's length, referring to it in the third person, as 'he'.

There is, however, some ambivalence in Emily's attitude. There is some acknowledgement of the beauty of daylight in the lines

CHECK THE POEM

Emily also uses the sea as a **metaphor** for the infinite in 'No coward soul is mine'. However, in 'Lines: I die, but when the grave shall press', she pictures life as 'a sea of gloom', and death as a safe anchorage. In 'A Death-Scene' (**stanzas** 4–6), the speaker asks her dying husband to delay crossing 'the eternal sea' and questions whether there are 'Eden Isles beyond'.

QUESTION

How significant is Emily's description of the sun as a male figure, 'arrow-straight ... fierce ... blazing', intruding into her bedroom?

'Restored our Earth to joy' (2) and 'steep in gold the misty dale' (27). Her glowing pillow, the birds singing in the wood, and the 'fresh winds' (36) are all appealing features. Even the murmuring flies – a lively realistic detail, and a reminder of ordinary everyday life – have a certain charm. It is as if the poet is torn between her love of nature, lit by daylight, and her thirst for the inner life and her mystical sense of unity, nurtured by night. She seems to feel that she must forego the joys of daylight, and perhaps by implication those of individual consciousness, in order to be one with the infinite. She seems to be torn between the natural world and the spiritual.

In the final stanza the poet makes a connection between human suffering and daylight, suggesting that suffering is caused by the alienation of individual human consciousness from the undifferentiated infinite. She prays that she may live entirely in the infinite. Up until now, each stanza has contained a complete sentence, which has helped to produce a firm sense of structure in the poem. Emily breaks this pattern in the final stanza, which continues the sentence begun in the penultimate one, bringing the poem to a swelling and satisfying close.

GLOSSARY

12	petrel	bird that spends most of its time at sea

'NO COWARD SOUL IS MINE'

- The poet states her belief in a personal God.
- She rejects conventional creeds and asserts the existence of a single divine spirit animating the universe.

In this remarkably assured statement of a very personal faith, Emily asserts the validity of her personal vision and her complete dismissal of conventional religious creeds, which, she says, cannot shake her from her personal faith in immortality. Expanding on this, she adds

QUESTION

W. B. Yeats (1865–1939) wrote: 'a poet writes always of his personal life, in his finest work, out of its tragedy, whatever it be, remorse, lost love, or mere loneliness.' Elsewhere he said, 'all that is personal soon rots.' How far do you feel the Brontës' lives are relevant to a study of their poetry?

that this divine spirit pervades all time and space. It is eternal and infinite, and embraces all existence. Given this, there is no room for Death in her philosophy, since all life is contained within this indestructible spirit.

COMMENTARY

In contemporary Western society, which tends to see religious faith, or the lack of it, as being a matter for individual conscience, 'No coward soul is mine' seems less remarkable as a statement than it might have done in British society in the time of the Brontës. Here was the twenty-nine-year-old daughter of a country vicar, daring to assert the sufficiency of her personal concept of 'God within my breast'. Not only that, she utterly rejects organised religion – the 'thousand creeds/ That move men's hearts' (9–10).

There is, for a start, a criticism implied by her numbering them in this way – surely not all thousand can be correct; moreover, she perceives them as forces which might actually undermine faith in God rather than strengthening it. Her sentence spans stanzas 3 and 4, so that she is actually saying that these creeds are 'vain ... To waken doubt in one/ Holding so fast by thy infinity' (11, 14). In other words, they cannot undermine her personal faith in the infinite. At the same time, the sentence is very long, and it is not strictly grammatical to call something 'Worthless ... To waken doubt' (11, 13). This suggests that she is not simply saying they cannot rock her faith, but that they are in themselves 'Worthless as withered weeds'. The image, strengthened by the alliteration, suggests that these creeds are outdated or dead – and even healthy weeds have little value! She goes on to compare them with 'froth' (12) floating on the sea emphasising their superficiality relative to the sea (a symbol of infinity), which surrounds the rock of faith on which she is anchored.

The phrase 'coward soul' (1) comes from a more conventionally Christian ode by Hester Chapone. Whereas Chapone rejects the idea of finding God in oneself as 'impious Pride', and takes Christ as her model, Emily is defiantly self-possessed. We see this even in her variation of the largely iambic metre of the poem in the third line, in which sense and form force us to emphasise the 'I' at the start of the line. She also varies the metre to emphasise 'Vain' in line 9. Perhaps concerned for her sister's salvation, when Charlotte edited this poem she made significant changes to the wording and the capitalisation, making it more conventionally Christian. Here are the final two stanzas in her version:

> Though earth and man were gone,
> And suns and universes ceased to be,
> And Thou were left alone,
> Every existence would exist in Thee.
>
> There is not room for Death,
> Nor atom that his might could render void:
> Thou – THOU art Being and Breath,
> And what THOU are may never be destroyed.

In Emily's version, 'earth and moon' stand for the entire universe, but, significantly, they are not living things: to her, what has once lived cannot die. Charlotte's substitution of 'man' for 'moon' disrupts this idea and makes the meaning more localised. Her repetition and capitalisation of 'thou', and the omission of the word 'Since' also make the last two lines a more conventionally Christian paean of praise rather than a continuation of the argument for continuing life. This version of God promulgated by Charlotte is at odds with Emily's, in which God's spirit 'Changes, sustains, dissolves, creates and rears' (20) in a never-ending cycle of creation and destruction.

ANNE BRONTË

THE BLUEBELL

- The poet comments on the spirit of the bluebell.
- She recalls a time when a bluebell moved her to tears.

The poet comments appreciatively on the spirit of individual flowers, and on the great happiness they give her. She recollects a

> **CONTEXT**
>
> Emily Brontë's idea of a deity producing a recurring cycle of creation, preservation and destruction is in line with Hindu philosophy, in which Brahma is a creator god, Vishnu is the Preserver, and Shiva is the Destroyer.

CHECK THE POEM

Like 'The Bluebell', Anne's poem 'The Consolation' explores her longing for home and familiar faces. However, whereas 'The Bluebell' suggests that happiness is gone for ever, in 'The Consolation' she is comforted by knowing that somewhere there is still a home where she is loved.

CHECK THE POEM

Romantic and early **Victorian** poets often wrote about flowers, usually associating them with spring. See, for example, John Clare (1793–1864), 'The Dying Child', which contains the lines 'His little hands, when flowers were seen,/ Were held for the bluebell'. See also Clare's most famous collection, *The Rural Muse* (1835).

time when, wandering happily down a flowery lane near the sea, on a sunny day, she saw a bluebell and was moved to tears. She explains that the flower reminded her of happy childhood times now past.

COMMENTARY

This poem has a simple eloquence, like the bluebell which it describes. It displays Anne's characteristic love of flowers, as well as her general sense of being lonely and unappreciated. Interestingly, the poem was written when she had been working as a governess at Thorp Green for some months. The penultimate stanza seems to refer to her employment, one of 'anxious toil and strife' (44) in which she is unthanked by her 'heartless' employers and their associates (41–2). However, the incident she describes occurs during a briefly happy respite 'when I led a toilsome life/ So many leagues away' (11). If she wrote this poem at Thorp Green, she must be recollecting a previous unhappy time away from her beloved home. Her sense of isolation at Thorp Green must have stirred her old feelings.

Whatever the exact circumstances of the poem's composition, it makes a satisfying narrative. Its opening statement borders on animism, claiming, as it does, that every flower has its own spirit. The poem can be compared with Emily's 'The bluebell is the sweetest flower', in which the flower also evokes feeling. Both sisters find the bluebell moving; Anne says it 'fills my softened heart with bliss' (7), but in her poem the bliss itself induces sadness through the memory of happiness lost.

Anne displays a sensitivity to the flower itself as a living thing. It is 'a little trembling flower,/ A single sweet bluebell' (27–8), a 'lovely floweret' (47), the simplicity of her words showing her uncomplicated appreciation. She captures some of the sense of magic that a flower might create for a sensitive child when she recalls how 'bluebells seemed like fairy gifts,/ A prize among the flowers' (35).

The rhythms of the poem are appropriately light and easy, and the ideas flow, on the whole, in a well-ordered sequence. However, there is a certain inconsequentiality in stanza 5. The 'lofty hill' (17) and the sea are not significant except as background details, and they bear no relation to the second two lines of the stanza. Similarly, although the way in which she gives a voice to the bluebell in the final stanza is fairly effective, and can be compared with Emily's 'The Night-Wind' (in which the wind speaks), the final line seems a little unnecessary, as it explains what was already quite clear from the earlier stanzas.

GLOSSARY

| 10 | league obsolete unit of distance, normally three miles |
| 43 | weal well-being |

LINES WRITTEN AT THORP GREEN

- The poet tells how summer must turn to winter before she will be able to go home.
- She says that winter at home is sweeter than summer to one away from home.

The central idea of this poem is simple but appealing. Anne observes that summer, pleasant though it is, must fade and give way to winter before the time comes when she is due to return to her beloved home. Structurally speaking, she comments on one main feature of summer in each of the first three stanzas, then finally compares the paradoxical sweetness of winter, to one who is at home, with the lesser sweetness of summer.

COMMENTARY

The central idea of the poem hinges on the interesting paradox of summer ordinarily seeming preferable to winter, yet the poet wanting it to pass so that the time will come for her return home. In describing this, she creates a strong impression of what home means to her. The implied inner sense of warmth, comfort and security that it offers is effectively contrasted with the 'long dark nights, and landscape drear' (23) in the outside world.

 CHECK THE POEM

'Lines Written at Thorp Green' may be compared to Emily's 'Loud without the wind was roaring', insofar as it conveys a strong sense of time passing by describing the seasonal changes in nature.

CHECK THE NET
See **http://mick-armitage.staff.shef.ac.uk/anne/bronte.html** for an informative site focusing on Anne, which also includes a tour of Thorp Green.

The development of ideas is similar in each stanza. In the first, Anne focuses on the sun, subtly personified, since 'genial' (1) normally describes a good-humoured character. She describes its cheering effect on her 'drooping spirit' (2), and the 'cold and silent' state (3) it must reach before the time comes when she will be happy. The next two stanzas follow a similar pattern. The breeze, personified as 'whispering' (7), cools her brow, but must turn to a wild and piercing winter wind before she is happy. Finally, the flowers she loves so much, and even the green leaves of summer, must fade and decay. There is no need to reiterate words to the effect of '…before I am happy', since this idea is now established.

This clever matching of the sequence of ideas in each stanza is complemented by the metre of the poem. The first rhyming couplet suggests the sweetness of summer, and the third line introduces the necessity of its ending in order for the longed-for return home to come. This third line then rhymes with the final line of the stanza. In the first two stanzas this links the two apparently opposed ideas of winter and happiness. The sense is pleasingly varied in the third stanza, since, as noted above, we now assume the '…before I am happy'.

The final stanza rounds off the poem, going one step further in sense than the earlier stanzas, in the claims it makes for the sweetness of winter to one at home, which she capitalises, 'Home' (24), for emphasis.

GLOSSARY

14	verbena	wild plant with white flowers

DESPONDENCY

- The poet writes of her sense of spiritual lethargy.
- She reflects on times in the past when she has felt intense religious fervour.
- She speaks of her wavering faith and prays to Jesus to save her.

Anne, perhaps the most devoutly Christian of the three sisters, chastises herself in this poem for spiritual regression. She recalls times when she wept in sorrow for her sins, vowed to do better, and felt 'so full of love,/ So strong in spirit' (21–2) that it seemed she would always feel alive with religious passion. Now, by comparison, her spirit is 'Drowsy and dark … Heavy and dull as lead' (3–4). She concludes with a more positive assertion that she can still pray, and appeals to Jesus to help her.

COMMENTARY

The vigorous but rather rigid metre of this uncompromising poem conveys a sense of anger and self-recrimination. The poet is clearly exasperated by her own lack of connection with God, and even more by her inability to feel any strong emotion. In non-religious terms we might see her as being depressed and unable to feel any enthusiasm or inspiration. The language she uses points to darkness, heaviness and bondage. The word order of 'Drowsy and dark my spirit lies' (3) emphasises the adjectives and uses alliteration to accentuate the sense of dull heaviness. So great is her sense of heaviness that she feels herself to be in 'iron chains' (7).

Set against this language of heaviness and bondage is the idea of freeing her spirit (8) and rising up: she speaks of how she raised her hands 'on high' in prayer (11). The adjectives she uses to describe her former state are very different from those describing her current heaviness of soul. Then, she felt 'fervent zeal,/An earnest grief and strong desire' (14–15).

The poem seems to sway between these two extremes – of dullness and fervour. Even after recalling her former fervour, she admits how many times she has strayed and forgotten God. After this, she reaches the poem's low point in the penultimate stanza, before ending with renewed resolution and humility.

 CHECK THE POEM
The metaphysical poet George Herbert (1593–1633) wrote many prayer-like poems. One in which he speaks of feeling distanced from God, comparable to Anne's 'Despondency', is 'Denial', which begins: 'When my devotions could not pierce/ Thy silent ears;/ Then was my heart broken, as was my verse' (available online and in Helen Gardner, ed., *The Metaphysical Poets*, Penguin Classics, 1972).

Peaks College

Learning Resource Centre
Tel: 0114 2602462

IN MEMORY OF A HAPPY DAY IN FEBRUARY

IN MEMORY OF A HAPPY DAY IN FEBRUARY

CONTEXT

Anne's joy in being able to say 'I **knew that my redeemer lived'** must be seen in the context of her struggle with the Calvinist beliefs to which she had been exposed by her aunt. Calvinism is a branch of Protestantism originated by the French reformer John Calvin (1509–64). It emphasises the sinful nature of humanity, and holds that human beings are damned unless saved by God's mercy. Extreme Calvinism holds that God has already ordained who will enter heaven ('the elect') or hell, and that humans are powerless to alter their fate. See Anne's poem 'A Word to the "Elect"' (in *Selected Poems*, ed. Stevie Davies, Carcanet, 1999).

- The poet thanks God for an experience of spiritual transcendence.
- She describes the experience in personal terms.

The poet thanks God for granting her a joyful experience of religious transcendence or illumination. She goes on to describe the experience, which characteristically occurred outdoors, in nature. She describes having glimpsed divine truths expressed in the physical world, and in the 'moral world' (29). This poem is very much a confirmation of a personal, loving God, not a remote deity.

COMMENTARY

Although nature itself is not the primary focus of this poem, it seems significant that the experience described takes place on a bright, windy day in February. It is a time when Anne would be noticing winter beginning to give way to spring, a time of optimism and revival. We know, too, that she tended to feel happy and invigorated on this sort of day. Her 'Lines Composed in a Wood on a Windy Day' has something of the same jubilant mood, although without the mystical experience, and both poems mention sun shining on 'withered grass' (line 7 of this 'In Memory of a Happy Day in February' and line 5 of 'Lines Composed in a Wood on a Windy Day'). This would seem to be a symbol of hope.

The experience Anne so confidently describes can be compared with Emily's account of a mystical experience in 'The Prisoner'. However, it is characteristic of the two sisters that, while Emily's account is more enigmatic and not overtly Christian, Anne's experience is set firmly within the framework of Christian belief. Emily speaks of 'the Invisible; the Unseen', but Anne speaks in more conventional terms: 'Heaven!' (24), 'God on high' (25), 'all His works displayed' (28). Similarly, her references to 'His glory', 'His wisdom' and 'His mercy' (30–2) are Victorian Christian commonplaces. The first line of the penultimate stanza is a slight rephrasing of 'I know that my redeemer liveth', an assertion of faith often quoted from the Old Testament (Job 19:25). Even the capitalisation of the personal pronoun for God, 'His', and the assumption that God is male, is a convention that Emily avoids. Even in her most overtly religious poem, 'No Coward Soul is Mine', she does not use 'He', and even when she addresses her God directly, she does not capitalise 'thou', as Anne does in her first line.

The very personal and confident tone of Anne's poem can be seen in the number of lines that begin with the word 'I', as in 'I was alone ...' (5). The tone is generally very positive, both in language and metre. A number of words relate to light in some way: 'The sun shone' (7), 'glow' (10), 'bright prosperity' (19), 'illumined by a ray of light' (23), 'I saw His glory shine' (30). This brightness is in contrast to the 'Deep secrets of His providence/ In darkness long concealed' (33–4).

> **CONTEXT**
>
> The line 'I know that my redeemer liveth' was famous, even in the Brontës' day, as the title of an aria in *Messiah* by George Frideric Handel (1685–1789).

> **GLOSSARY**
>
> 41   **Redeemer** one who saves from damnation – Jesus Christ

THE CAPTIVE DOVE

- Anne addresses a captive dove, identifying with its captivity and lack of a mate.

Anne speaks to a captive dove, pitying its lack of freedom to fly and enjoy the delights of the air and the surrounding countryside. She devotes two stanzas to the idea that, if it had a female dove for a mate, it could be happy even in captivity. In fact, by the final stanza, the focus has shifted from the bird's lack of liberty to its lack of a loving partner.

COMMENTARY

Anne wrote this poem while working as a governess at Thorp Green, where we know she felt unhappy and lonely, so it seems likely that she strongly identified with the captive dove. In fact she

CONTEXT

The New Testament uses the dove as a **symbol** of the Holy Spirit. See Matthew 3:16 and Mark 1:10. It is also possible that Anne had, in the back of her mind, the story from Greek myth of the goddess Hera taking pity on Zeus when he disguised himself as a dove in order to woo her.

ascribes human feelings to the bird. She assumes that whatever sound it makes is a 'plaintive moan' (2), that it gazes 'into the distant sky' (7), presumably thinking about flying up there, that it feels 'despair' (12), and that its 'little drooping heart' (18) would be cheered by having 'One faithful dear companion' (22). The wanderings she imagines it enjoying also suggest those that she would enjoy herself, especially in the mention of 'the rolling sea' (15), perhaps reflecting her own sense of being trapped in her role as a governess. However, the poem is saved from sentimentality by Anne's sincere compassion for the bird, even if she does think of it in overly human terms. The poem also works on a symbolic level, since the dove is a Christian symbol of the Holy Spirit, and has often been used, by extension, as a symbol of spiritual liberation.

GLOSSARY

14	mead meadow

A REMINISCENCE

- The poet regrets the passing of someone buried in the church, yet rejoices in this person's cheerfulness.

CONTEXT

William Weightman died of cholera in 1842, aged only twenty-eight. There has been speculation that Anne was in love with him, but there is no real evidence for this, and the tone of 'A Reminiscence' is not that of a bereaved lover.

Anne regrets the death of someone she apparently knew and towards whom she felt much affection. She thinks of how this person lies buried beneath the church floor, and in the second half of the poem takes comfort in the fact that such a person has lived, albeit briefly.

COMMENTARY

This short and quite straightforward poem could be addressed to Anne's father's curate, William Weightman, but we cannot be sure. The fairly light tone suggests that this person was not someone to whom Anne was closely attached, but rather someone with whom she was casually familiar on a daily basis. The poem has a light touch, for a reminiscence, focusing on the good spirits and even good looks ('a form so angel fair', 14) of the deceased. Their good humour is described simply: 'Thy sunny smile' (2). Anne anticipates pacing the floor above his or her grave, and compares the 'cold, damp stone' (5) with the warm heart of the deceased. The second stanza can be compared with Emily's 'Remembrance', which also pictures the deceased '[c]old in the earth', but which expresses a tortured sense of bitter loss, rather than the relatively casual (though warm) affection of Anne's poem.

Anne makes an interesting distinction in the final stanza between the deceased's 'soul so near divine', their 'form, so angel fair' (13–14), and their light heart. This stanza runs on in sense from the previous one. Together they make a fitting epitaph.

? QUESTION

In 'A Reminiscence', Anne takes comfort in the fact that someone so good has lived. How does this compare with the consolation taken by Charlotte in 'On the Death of Emily Jane Brontë' or by Branwell in 'Epistle From a Father to a Child in Her Grave'?

HOME

- The poet observes a woodland scene on a bright winter's day.
- She wishes she could be in her native countryside near her home instead.
- She comments on the attractive grounds and rooms of the mansion where she is living, but wishes she could be back in her humble home.

As in 'Lines Written at Thorp Green' and 'The Consolation', the major theme of this poem is Anne's homesickness. She acknowledges the attractions of the countryside around her, the fine gardens – presumably of Thorp Green, and the rooms of the mansion where she is employed – but expresses her heartfelt wish that she could be home instead, even if its surrounding countryside is bleak and cold, and its garden neglected.

COMMENTARY

The sentiment of this poem is simple. Anne paints an attractive picture of the scene around her, notwithstanding the fact that it is winter. All seems benign: the ivy is 'brightly glistening' (1), the

CONTEXT

Anne wrote 'Home' while at Thorp Green, where she worked as a governess between 1840 and 1845. It was only forty miles from Haworth, but the limited transport of the time meant that she was only able to make rare visits home.

beech trees reflect the sun's 'silver rays' (4), the skies are 'softly smiling' (6). The wind 'sighs' and 'thunders' (8–9), but this in itself does not deter Anne. Indeed she would gladly trade this relatively soft countryside for the barrenness and 'colder breezes' (12) of her native Haworth.

Anne effectively brings to life the pleasant and stately walks of the garden at Thorp Green. Everything here is tidy and manicured – 'borders trim,/ And velvet lawns' (19–20), in contrast with the 'knotted grass neglected' and 'weeds' (23–4) of the garden at Haworth.

In contrast with her poem 'The Bluebell', she makes no complaint about the people she lives with, or even about missing her loved ones. Instead, the focus here is entirely on her longing for home itself. Appropriately, then, she ends with a final appeal, even capitalising the word 'HOME' (28) for emphasis, and ending with an exclamation mark.

CHECK THE POEM

Anne's poem 'If This Be All' is a fitting footnote to 'Dreams', and reads almost as a continuation of it. She speaks of dreaming of bliss and waking **'to weary woe'**, of love keeping **'so far away'**, and of wanting to share feelings that she is forced to keep to herself. Two other poems by Anne, 'Oh, they have robbed me of the hope' and 'The Arbour', have something of this same sense of disappointment that seems to have been a feature of Anne's emotional life.

DREAMS

- The poet comments on the consolations of imagination.
- She says that she can imagine the joys of motherhood – until she is forced to remember that she is unloved.
- She asks God if she is doomed to remain loveless.

This is a poignant poem, in which Anne begins by speaking appreciatively of her power of imagination. She imagines the joy of being a mother, then speaks of her misery on returning to the consciousness that she is alone and unloved. Addressing God, she asks if her naturally warm affections will only ever find expression in fantasy.

COMMENTARY

Although in other poems Anne often describes herself as lonely, here she says, thanks to 'fancy', 'I seldom feel myself alone' (2–3).

However, she immediately conjures up an imagined picture of herself as the loving mother of a baby. Her description is touching, as she speaks of the bliss of knowing the child depends on her, knowing that she is 'beloved at last' (18), and that she need no longer live a 'life of solitude' (20). These lines may, of course, relate to a hoped-for husband – her imaginary baby's father. Real mothers may point out that caring for a baby has its more challenging side, too, but it is understandable that Anne is selective in her fantasy.

After such an account of motherhood, it comes as a shock to the reader, as well as to Anne herself, to be plunged back into stark consciousness of the 'dreary void' that she actually inhabits (24), whether by waking from actual dreams – if we take the title literally – or by coming back to reality out of a daydream.

Her plea in the final stanza is especially touching. She stops short of accusing God of giving her a loving heart and then denying it expression, yet her words do convey a sense of the seemingly cruel irony of her situation.

LAST LINES

- The poet prays for fortitude in the face of her impending death.

This poem represents Anne's response to being diagnosed as having tuberculosis, shortly after Emily had died of the disease. It is a frank and courageous admission of her situation, combined with a passionate prayer to God to help her face the suffering and likely death to come.

COMMENTARY

This poem is full of a brave humility. Like 'A Prayer' and 'The Penitent', it is strongly Christian in tone. Anne speaks of the 'dreadful darkness' closing in on her (1), her weariness, the 'days of passive misery' (38), yet she never complains or betrays self-pity. Her sorrow is as much for the death of Emily as for her own

QUESTION

Do you think Anne is referring to the baby in **stanzas 4 and 5**, or its father? Is she fantasising about being a single parent, or is she just reluctant to make her desire for a man explicit?

CHECK THE POEM

In one of her Gondal poems, 'Song to A. A.', Emily imagines motherhood, the **narrator** of the poem addressing a verse lullaby to her baby rocking on the ocean waves.

CHECK THE POEM

One might compare Anne's humble attitude to God, and towards her desperate plight, to Branwell's attitude, as expressed in 'Oh Thou, whose beams were most withdrawn'. This was written at a time when he had, objectively speaking, no special personal problems. Nonetheless he prays for 'one short space of rest/ Ere I go home to dust and worms' (15–16) and complains of being 'prostrate 'neath despair' (22).

impending doom. Her attitude is almost saintly. She asks for God's comfort, prays that she will be able to avoid sin, gives thanks for her past joys, and begs for the 'humble patience' to accept suffering (54).

The language of the poem does, of course, reflect Anne's suffering vividly: 'all this world of blinding mist' (5); the balanced **alliteration** of 'watch the painful night/ And wait the weary day' (27–8), and the repeated 'Crushed with sorrow, worn with pain' (42, 46). (These two **stanzas** are so similar as to make one wonder whether Anne actually intended to delete one of them.) Yet the tone is surprisingly calm, and even logical, considering Anne's situation. It may be that the tight rhyme and rigid **metre** are her way of holding her feelings in check, but they could also be construed as giving a sense of determination.

Anne begins by praying for help in bearing her lot, speaks of her former hopes, resigning herself to their loss. She reasons that, since she has benefited from God's blessings, she must also accept suffering. She is aware, too, of 'the sins/ That ever wait on suffering' (49–50) – presumably such sins as impatience, self-pity and even despair – and prays for help in overcoming them. Finally, in the last three stanzas, she considers the possible outcomes. She may die soon or later: 'thus early to depart/ Or yet awhile to wait' (59–60). She may be spared: 'If thou shouldst bring me back to life' (61). Or she may be about to die: 'Should Death be standing at the gate' (65). These last stanzas give an impression of a woman who has carefully thought through an appalling situation and has reconciled herself to all possible outcomes.

GLOSSARY

| 18 | portioned | apportioned, allotted |

EXTENDED COMMENTARIES

CHARLOTTE BRONTË, THE TEACHER'S MONOLOGUE

This poem is Charlotte's reflection on her feelings at the end of a day's teaching at Roe Head, and on her life as a whole. Charlotte was not especially unhappy teaching at Roe Head, and she liked the principal, Miss Wooler, but she found the work monotonous and missed having time to herself. In addition most of her income went towards financing Anne's education at the school, leaving her little or nothing to save towards improving her own situation. (For more on Charlotte and Roe Head, see **The Brontës lives and works: Education and early works**.)

QUESTION

'The Teacher's Monologue' is a very personal poem. Why then do you think Charlotte gives it such an impersonal title?

The beginning of the poem reflects the weariness Charlotte feels in relation to teaching, but also the relative pleasure of having the classroom to herself at the end of the working day. However, there is a gradual decline in the poem's mood, the poet passing from calm contentment to nostalgic thoughts of home, self-doubt, and anxieties about her family. In the second part of the poem, she realises that she has worked herself unintentionally into a mournful mood, and pulls herself up, only to relapse and give full voice to her gloomy pessimism.

The poem begins with a wonderful evocation of the sense of calm that can follow a demanding day, especially in a school classroom after the pupils have left. The rhythm here reflects the mood of 'mute tranquillity' (2). In particular, the lines 'I am as it is bliss to be,/ Still and untroubled' (4–5) have a wonderful simplicity, the emphasis in the second line falling on 'Still' because of its dactylic rhythm and the mid-line sentence-ending, necessitating a pause to match the pause in the poet's busy life. Her image of the day winging its way 'O'er waveless water, stirless tree' (7) is also very evocative.

The manner in which this quiet calm turns to more melancholic thoughts is insidious. The 'distant hill' (9) delicately painted as 'So faint, so blue, so far removed' (10), by its very distance leads her to think of her distant family, and to her childhood, her 'happiest hours' (17) spent 'among moors' (19) around her native Haworth. It seems characteristic of Charlotte, however, that even this happy thought leads quickly to a comparison of these times with her adulthood, in which 'life's first prime' has 'Decayed to dark anxiety' (19–20), the alliteration emphasising the leaden nature of the change.

Self-doubt follows. Charlotte worries that her inability to form close friendships with those around her may be owing to her 'narrow heart' (21) – one which in effect only has room in it for her own family. This leads her to deeper uncertainty: 'All the sweet thoughts' of family (27), on which she depends, seem to desert her. They seem unreal in the face of the harsh reality of her everyday life. Her distress is palpable: 'aching grief, so void and lone' (33). She personifies 'Joy and transient Sorrow shed' as the 'sun and rain' (36–7) that have nurtured the seeds of her hope, to yield a harvest that then seems to be mere illusion. In the third stanza, she tips over into anxiety, worrying about her family, their feared loss represented in the homely domestic metaphors of 'The hearth-fire quenched, the vacant chair' (46).

When the poet calls a halt to this downhill flood of feeling, she changes the metre of the poem, from lines of four stresses each (actually iambic quadrameter) to alternate lines of four and three stresses. This is a little more jaunty, and for a little more than a stanza she seems to take heart, saying that she had actually intended to sing 'a song that sweet and clear,/ Though haply sad, might flow' (57–8). However, even this lapses into the stark admission 'In vain I try; I cannot sing' (63), and she resorts to looking forward to death, the time when 'Repose shall toil repay' (70).

The last two stanzas of the poem become increasingly abstract as they lean more heavily on personification. Patience is 'weary with her yoke' (75), 'Health's elastic spring is broke' (77), Death is 'A welcome, wished-for friend' (88), and the poet finally calls on Reason, Patience and Faith (those great stand-bys of the troubled Victorian) to help her 'suffer to the end' (90). In calling on Reason she is harking back to the eighteenth-century 'Age of Enlightenment', a broad movement which coincided with the beginnings of the Industrial Revolution, and which developed the idea that human beings could pursue happiness through philosophy and the intellect. In appealing to Patience and Faith, however, she is summoning distinctly Christian virtues. Victorian Christianity placed special emphasis on the need to maintain a patient faith in the heavenly rewards awaiting the believer after death. Patience was especially required of women since they had so little opportunity to improve their lives by positive action. It seems that Charlotte expects no relief from suffering in this life, only in the hereafter. The bleakness of the abstract nouns she uses suggests that, despite her best intentions, the prospect is not a cheerful one.

This is a very introspective poem, and a very honest one, which shows how the poet's mind wanders from quiet contemplation to a range of insecurities, the weightiest of which is that her life will be ultimately unfulfilling – that she is doomed merely to fade away after a life of empty longing. The poem's universal appeal lies in the extent to which these anxieties are the concerns of humanity at large.

GLOSSARY		
13	yon azure brow	that blue hill over there
16	Thitherward tending	in that direction
51	air	tune
58	haply	perhaps
59	strain	tune

PATRICK BRANWELL BRONTË, EPISTLE FROM A FATHER TO A CHILD IN HER GRAVE

This dignified poem, addressed to a dead infant, expresses what are generally thought to be Branwell's feelings on contemplating the early death of his own illegitimate daughter. The word 'epistle' can simply mean a letter, but here it refers to a poem in the form of a letter, a poetic form dating from Roman times. Many other poets have written epistles. John Keats, for example, wrote 'Epistle to My Brother George', and Robert Burns (with whose work Branwell was familiar, as we know from 'Penmaenmawr') also wrote a

CHECK THE POEM

Branwell's poem might be compared with a much shorter, but very moving, poem to a dead son, 'On My First Son', by Ben Jonson (1572–1637). Jonson, like Branwell, takes some comfort in his child having escaped the woes of the world: '... For why/ Will man lament the state he should envy?/ To have so soon 'scaped world's and flesh's rage,/ And if no other misery, yet age!'

number of epistles, such as 'Epistle to Colonel De Peyster'. Such epistles vary a great deal in style, though they have in common the fact that they are addressed to one person. They tend to adopt a personal tone, but they do not necessarily focus exclusively on the person whom they address. Branwell's poem 'The man who will not know another' is just as much an epistle as 'Epistle From a Father to a Child in Her Grave', though it is not called one.

In this poem, Branwell is addressing a child whom he probably never really knew, yet for whom he feels a natural kinship. The basic content of the poem is fairly easy to summarise. The child is beyond earthly cares; she will never know her father; had she known him, she would never have been able to relate his suffering to her own very limited and largely blissful infant experience; men would stigmatise her for being born to an unmarried mother, yet she was innocent and beautiful, and he can only rejoice now that she will never suffer like him.

The heroic couplets seem appropriate to Branwell's subject, giving it a fitting sense of gravity. It is also very much the epic style to draw out these relatively simply ideas into a fairly lengthy poem. It is more Branwell's personal style that, although addressed to the child, much of the poem is really about him, and especially about his own suffering. This is particularly true in stanzas 4 and 5, in which Branwell compares the infant's brief life, lived 'in a bed of roses' (50), with his own, plagued by 'miseries each hour new dread creating' (40).

CHECK THE POEM

The opening of this poem, with its references to spring, may be compared with Chaucer's opening to the 'General Prologue' of *The Canterbury Tales* (1400), which also speaks of sweet April showers giving life to spring flowers.

Branwell's attempt to bring epic stature to the poem can be seen in stanza 1, in which he expansively addresses himself to the child. He is writing to her 'from Earth' (1), which he describes in a way appropriate to his youthful and innocent subject, in terms of spring flowers. She, presumably, is in heaven, although he dwells more on her simply being impervious to events on earth. She is even less touched by them than the bravest of soldiers ('son of Mars', the god of war, 8), or the most equanimous of philosophers ('Stoic's long ago', 9).

In the second stanza, Branwell acknowledges that his child will never read what he is writing, however much his heart bleeds for her. He cannot resist a comment here on how others misjudge him: 'The heart that many think a worthless stone,/ But which oft aches for some beloved one' (17–18). He follows this with an extended metaphor comparing the child to the pre-dawn twilight, only the morning star (perhaps Venus) feebly illuminating her life. He warns, at the same time, of troubles yet to come in adult life – the 'veil of thundercloud' (30) over the sun.

The fourth stanza paints a dreamy imaginary picture of how the child might have seen him 'On skies of azure blue and waters green,/ Melting to mist amid the summer sheen' (37–8). The idealised blue sky and summer mist are contrasted with his actual sufferings, and particularly his 'troubled pleasures soon chastised by fear' (42), which probably refers to his clandestine affair with Lydia Robinson, his employer's wife (see **Background: The Brontës' lives and works**), although the identity of the mother of Branwell's illegitimate child is unknown.

Branwell goes on to paint quite a touching picture of the child's world, focused entirely on its mother's breast. With no small idealism, and perhaps some envy, he compare the child with someone reclining on a 'bed of roses' with only 'marbled skies above' and 'breezes whispering in the grove' (50–2). Rather oddly, he says that this life was not far removed from 'childhood's grave' (48). The picture of peace is compared with his own life sufferings, imaged as 'rough rocks' and stormy weather (56–7), and by 'that drear country called "The Life of Man"' (61). He hints at a determining power in the 'mysterious hand' (60) that draws up the plan of that country.

Finally, Branwell reflects on the way in which an illegitimate child would be stigmatised, whereas he, its father, might not be: yet she was the innocent one. He concludes with the sentiment often found in the Brontës' poetry – that the dead are better off, and that the living can take comfort in that. This sentiment is also found in Charlotte's 'On the Death of Emily Jane Brontë'. It might be compared with Anne's rather more positive view in 'A Reminiscence', in which she takes comfort in the fact that the person the poem addresses has lived.

CONTEXT

The phrase 'troubled pleasures soon chastised by fear' is quoted almost exactly from Homer's *Iliad*, Book 6, as translated by Alexander Pope (1688–1744). Andromache soothes her baby: 'The troubled pleasure soon chastised by fear,/ She mingled with a smile a tender tear.' Branwell also uses the phrase in a letter to Francis Grundy to describe his guilty lovemaking with Lydia Robinson.

 CHECK THE POEM

In the phrase 'The Life of Man', Branwell may have had in mind a poem of that name by Sir Francis Bacon (1561–1626), which portrays human life as one of grim suffering: 'The World's a bubble, and the Life of Man/ Less than a span:/ In his conception wretched, from the womb/ So to the tomb.'

> **GLOSSARY**
>
> 9   **Stoic** follower of the ancient Greek school of philosophy which taught that life was predetermined and that human beings should reconcile themselves to their fate

EMILY JANE BRONTË, THE PRISONER

This much-praised narrative poem, published as 'A Fragment' because it was originally taken from a longer poem, can be interpreted on a number of levels. On the material level its narrator, a man in a position of power and authority, recalls paying a casual visit to his dungeons accompanied by his jailor. The fact that he is *recalling* this visit is important, as he is now – in the 'present' time of his narration – what one might call, in Coleridge's words from *The Ancient Mariner*, 'a sadder and a wiser man'. This is why he expresses regret for his former callousness: 'God forgive my youth; forgive my careless tongue' (9). His regret primes us to take his narrative seriously, and to feel more compassion for his prisoners than he evidently did before hearing the story of his female prisoner. The rather stately iambic hexameter of the poem, with its caesura after the third stress in each line, also demands that we pay close attention to the slow unfolding of the narrative.

The male narrator, in his recollected narrative, scoffs at his captives, but is struck by the saintly and unworldly manner of one young woman. She has no interest in being freed, and in fact looks forward to death as her final liberation. She describes in detail the visionary experience that she has each night, when she is carried out of the confines of the self, transported to a place of unutterable peace and harmony – only to find herself, at the moment of union with the infinite, falling back into the confines of her body. The narrator, and even the jailor, are stunned to silence by her account, and leave her to her expected death. Thus the whole poem is a framed narrative, a story within a story, like *Wuthering Heights*, which is narrated partly by Lockwood and partly by Nelly Dean.

On a symbolic level, the imprisonment of the young woman represents the imprisonment of the spirit in its earthly body. This is

CONTEXT

'The Prisoner' is a Gondal narrative, and was taken from a longer poem called 'Julian M. and A. G. Rochelle'. In the original version, Julian is visiting his dungeons when he encounters Rochelle, who turns out to be his childhood playmate. He falls in love with her, she accepts his offer of freedom, he nurses her through a long illness, and she eventually comes to love him.

brought home powerfully in lines 53–6, in which she seems to describe a descent from spiritual heights to earthly depths. There is a sense of descending stages: first hearing, then eyesight, then consciousness of the body's mechanics, then thinking – all return. The process is completed with the terrible finality of 'The soul to feel the flesh, and the flesh to feel the chain' (56). This is both the physical chain of her fetters, and the invisible chain that binds her soul to her body so long as she is alive. Perhaps the 'triple walls' within which the prisoners are said to be confined (11) reflect the confines of body, mind and soul.

We can even look at the poem from a third perspective, regarding its three characters and its dungeon setting as aspects of the human psyche. If the young woman represents the spirit's urge towards liberation from the self and union with the infinite, then the male narrator represents the authority of society that insists on the individual playing his or her part in the world. This fits with the low voice and 'his aspect bland and kind', masking a soul 'hard as hardest flint' (25–6), perhaps reflecting the Victorian Establishment, laying claim to Christian charity but in reality being both self-serving and extremely punitive towards anyone failing to conform to its social norms (see **Historical and social background**). The jailor can be seen as the lowest expression of this oppressive authority, or even as representing the demands of the body itself.

For a relatively short text, there is considerable characterisation in the poem. The male narrator reveals both his past character and his present character by his comments on himself. He describes himself as straying 'idly' in his dungeons, 'Reckless of the lives wasting there away' (1–2), expressing both his lack of compassion at the time and his present-day censure of his younger self. He notes that the warder 'dared not say me nay' (3), indicating that he was, even then, a man of authority, not to be trifled with. The jailor is an unsavoury character. At first merely 'sullen' (8), he joins the narrator in scoffing at the prisoner in stanza 6 and calling her 'fond, dreaming wretch' (22). However, he seems to be an astute judge of character when he comments on his master appearing to be 'bland and kind', while actually being 'hard as hardest flint' (25–6).

CHECK THE BOOK

The jailor's description of the narrator's 'aspect bland and kind' masking a soul 'hard as hardest flint' makes one think of the character of St John Rivers in Charlotte Brontë's novel *Jane Eyre*. Rivers is a fiercely committed Christian, but shows little of the true compassion recommended by Christ.

CHECK THE BOOK

In 'The Prisoner' the chained prisoner represents the confines of the body. This idea is also suggested in *Wuthering Heights* when Catherine calls her body 'this shattered prison'. The jailor in the prison is similar to Joseph in *Wuthering Heights,* a grim moralist who does his best to restrict the freedom of the young Cathy and Heathcliff and punishes them for their transgressions.

QUESTION

How do you interpret 'Desire for nothing known in my maturer years'? Is the first meaning suggested here correct, or the second? Could both meanings be intended?

The character of the prisoner is disarming. She greets the jailor's rough words with 'a smile of almost scorn' (29). She reveals that her family have already perished – perhaps in war or somehow at the hands of the narrator, and she implies that her own life is already lost (31). She is too proud to 'weep and sue' for release (32). Moreover, she takes her nightly visitations as a sign that her own death will soon release her from captivity – both from her cell and from her body.

The prisoner's account of her mystical experience is remarkable, both in its message and its language. The poet personifies the prisoner's nightly experience as a male visitor, rather as she personifies the seductive wind in 'The Night-Wind'. A powerful sense of atmosphere is created in lines 37–40 by the alliteration of 'western winds ... wandering airs', the wonderful image of 'thickest stars', which suggests an intensifying of the stars, as if they are clustered together, and by the phrase 'clear dusk of heaven' (38), suggesting the clarity of the mystical vision. The oxymoronic 'tender fire' and the emotionally charged 'kill me with desire' (39–40) suggest the extraordinary and paradoxical nature of the experience, as well as hinting at something sexual.

This sense of paradox is continued in the next stanza. The prisoner is filled with 'Desire for nothing known in my maturer years' (41). This may mean a desire for an experience that she has not known since becoming an adult, or, as suggested by Derek Stanford in *Emily Bronte Her Life and Work* (co-written with Muriel Spark), it may mean a desire to experience *nothingness* – a desire which she has felt since becoming mature. She seems to suggest that Joy was quenched in her by the expectation of 'future tears' (42), and that, previously, she was uncertain of the origins of her flashes of inspiration. She experiences a 'soundless calm' (45), perhaps related to the 'peace of God that passeth all understanding' (Philippians 4:7). We have further oxymorons in 'Mute music ... unuttered harmony' (47). The climax of the poem is reached with an image of the prisoner's 'inward essence' seen metaphorically as a hawk or eagle, 'stooping' to its 'harbour' (50–51) – before she is pulled up short of final liberation. There is a wild abandonment of conventional Victorian morality in the penultimate stanza, in which the prisoner declares herself indifferent as to whether her vision is hellish or heavenly, providing it heralds death.

The 'framing' of the narrative is completed by the last stanza. Its language is suitably muted, matching the reaction of the male narrator and jailor to the prisoner's account. He quietly acknowledges that Heaven itself has overruled the sentence he himself passed on the prisoner, perhaps reflecting a belief that spiritual laws outweigh temporal or earthly ones. In our expectation that the prisoner will die, we are given a promise of closure. However, this is qualified by the feminine (unstressed) line endings of the final couplet, which, rather, suggest a straining *towards* closure, representing the prisoner's as yet unfulfilled yearning.

CHECK THE POEM

Milton's epic poem *Paradise Lost* describes the great gulf between heaven and hell. Satan is seen 'rowling in the fiery Gulfe/ Confounded though immortal' (Book 1, lines 52–3).

GLOSSARY		
1	crypts	underground vaults where bodies are buried (usually in a church)
4	say me nay	refuse me
10	flag-stones	large stone slabs on floor
52	gulph	(gulf) a yawning gap

CHECK THE BOOK

The language in lines 37–40 of 'The Prisoner' is reminiscent of the **oxymorons** in *Romeo and Juliet*, in which Romeo speaks of love as 'Feather of lead, bright smoke, cold fire, sick health' (I. 1. 178).

ANNE BRONTË, MEMORY

This finely crafted poem is characteristic of Anne's appreciation of nature, though its primary subject is the interaction between nature and her memory. Nature triggers memories, and at the same time her experiences of nature live on vividly in her memory. The poem describes a sunny summer's day replete with sensual attractions. However, she then dismisses these in favour of the memory of a single primrose, which pulls her soul away from the external world. This makes her think of how wonderful primroses seemed to her in childhood, which in turn makes her address an appeal to Memory, asking it to continue to remind her of all the things she loves – especially flowers and other natural things.

Becoming thoughtful towards the end of the poem, Anne asks Memory if it is actually childhood itself that is so divine, or whether in fact Memory makes it appear so in retrospect.

CHECK THE POEM

William Wordsworth's 'Intimations of Immortality from Recollections of Early Childhood' explores much more fully the same idea of the glory of childhood having passed away. Wordsworth also shares Anne Brontë's sense of being inspired by nature. One could, for example, compare her many flower-related poems with his 'Daffodils'. Her line 'From **earth, and air, and sky**' may be influenced by Wordsworth, reminding us of a line from 'A Slumber Did My Spirit Seal': 'Rolled round in earth's diurnal course,/ With rocks, and stones, and trees.'

Answering her own question, she concludes that the latter cannot be entirely the case, since Memory does not cast the same glamour over 'later pleasures' (47).

Anne begins by conjuring a generally pleasing and happy picture, with colour ('green fields', 2; 'sky of purest blue', 4) and gentle alliteration ('waving woods … winds wandered', 2–3). This sets the scene for a brief narrative, describing the experience she had on this day, which leads on to philosophical reflection. The phrase 'one sweet breath of memory/ Came gently wafting by' (8–9) suggests that she has smelt the primrose, though in fact this cannot be the case, since the primrose is a flower of spring. Rather, memory is perceived almost as a sense, perhaps related to the particular power of smell to evoke memories. This memory makes her willingly cut off from the external world of 'earth, and air, and sky' (12) to indulge her mind's eye.

The central part of the poem is really a paean of praise to memory, but also to nature, since three whole stanzas are given over to describing some of its many delights. Characteristically for Anne, the foremost of these are floral – the crocus, the wall-flower, the bluebell (given special favour), the daisy, the buttercup, the mountain star and heather. The flowers, mostly to be found in spring and summer, are balanced by description of winter – frost, snow, wild wind, and 'rippling waters' (36), showing that Anne loves nature in all its aspects, and not just its softer side.

Her consideration of whether childhood is divine, or memory makes it appear so, is interesting, though not entirely original. Her image of memory 'That haloes thus the past' (39) is well-chosen, since a halo, as an encircling light, is often depicted as marking out saints, and especially Christ – those who are divine. This is the 'holy light' of line 45. She acknowledges the occasional unhappiness of childhood, before concluding that memory alone cannot make the past seem divine: therefore, some of the sense of divinity, at least, must pertain to the consciousness of the child.

The metrical structure of the poem is slightly more complex than most of Anne's poems, having six lines in a stanza, rhyming *aabccb*.

This fits the more thoughtful tone of the poem. It also provides a pause at the end of the third line, which she uses in some stanzas to accentuate the development of her ideas. For example, in the penultimate stanza, the first three lines ask the question, and the remaining three lines answer it. In the final stanza, the first three lines are about 'our earliest joys' (44), while the final three lines compare them with 'our later pleasures'. Overall, this metre helps to create a sense of delicate balance in the poem which is characteristic of Anne's relatively calm and moderate temperament, in contrast with Emily's passion, Charlotte's longing, and Branwell's often rather melodramatic self-absorption.

 **QUESTION**

How far do you agree with Anne that there is something divine about childhood which is lost as we grow into adulthood?

PART THREE

CRITICAL APPROACHES

THEMES

LOSS

The overarching theme in the Brontës' poetry is loss – indeed, it encompasses almost all of the other themes they engage with – and can be found in so many of the poems. At a psychological level this may stem from the death of their mother, in 1821, followed by the deaths of their older sisters Maria and Elizabeth in 1825. In a spiritual sense, it may stem ultimately from the surviving Brontës' intimation of there being something better than this world, of which they have a kind of memory. Parted from it in this life, they can only hope to regain it in heaven, or in a fusion with the infinite that in this lifetime can only be transient.

CONTEXT

Mrs Maria Brontë died of cancer when Charlotte was five, Branwell four, Emily two and Anne only one year old.

This sense of loss, however, most obviously arises in those poems dealing with bereavement, whether real, as in Charlotte's heart-rending epitaphs to her sisters, 'On the Death of Emily Jane Brontë' and 'On the Death of Anne Brontë', or fictional, as in Emily's 'Remembrance'. Charlotte's two poems show her struggling to come to terms with overwhelming loss. In a sense, Emily's death only intensifies the feelings of inconsolable loneliness that Charlotte already has. She must now face 'life's lone wilderness' (15) without her sister. There is less intensity in 'On the Death of Anne Brontë', but also less hope of consolation. In the earlier poem, Charlotte focuses on the desperate comfort she wrings from the knowledge that Emily is now beyond suffering, and the hope that they will meet in heaven. In mourning Anne, although she thanks God for her release, she is beyond consolation.

Anne's poem 'A Reminiscence', commemorating the passing of someone unnamed, takes a very different approach to death, perhaps partly because the author had a less intimate relationship with the deceased. Still, it is typical of Anne's generally more hopeful outlook that she takes comfort in having known the subject of the poem, and in the very fact that he or she has lived: "Tis sweet to think that thou hast been' (12). This poem may be compared with Branwell's 'On Caroline'. This seems to speak of a fictional loss, albeit one emotionally informed by Branwell's own childhood bereavements. For the speaker there is no consolation, but here the focus is on the impossibility of forgetting.

The poem which deals with the terrible intractability of memory in bereavement most strikingly, however, is Emily's 'Remembrance'. The sense of loss here is appalling, but it is confronted sternly. The dead lover is described with brutal realism: 'Cold in the earth – and the deep snow piled above thee' (1). Moreover, the speaker cannot forget him even after fifteen years. Yet, although there is absolutely no consolation to be found, she has schooled herself to carry on living, simply because she must. To allow herself the 'divinest anguish' (31) of full memory would be to invite despair.

More generally in the Brontës' poems there is a sense of loss relating to the past. This may be to do with regrets for lost childhood intimacy, as hinted at in Charlotte's 'Retrospection', the loss of simple delight in the natural world, as in Anne's 'Memory' (in which she recollects her infant joy in a primrose), or the loss of childhood lightness of heart, as in Branwell's 'Death Triumphant': 'Have I the footsteps bounding free,/ The happy laugh of infancy?' (32–3).

Connected to this loss of the past is the homesickness of which all three sisters complain in their poems. Charlotte turns, in 'The Teacher's Monologue', from a calm contemplation of her surroundings to feelings of homesickness and anxieties for her family. She feels herself to be parted from 'all Earth holds for me' (14) and fears that her 'very home ... will soon be desolate' (41–2). Emily yearns for the moors of her homeland in 'The blue bell is the sweetest flower', while acknowledging that the sight of heather would only make her weep: 'I know how fast my tears would swell/ To see it smile today' (23–4). For Anne, the worst afflicted, the theme of homesickness arises in several poems. In 'The Bluebell', she longs for 'Those sunny days of merriment/ When heart and soul were free' (37–8); in 'Lines Written at Thorp Green', she thinks of how an entire winter must pass before she can go home; in 'The

> **? QUESTION**
>
> Many critics regard 'Remembrance' as Emily's best poem. How do you think it compares in quality with her other outstanding poems, such as 'The Prisoner', 'Stars' or 'The Night-Wind'?

Consolation', she finds comfort in there being 'though far away/ A home where heart and soul may rest' (19–20); and 'Home' ends with the heart-felt 'Oh, give me back my Home!' (28). Perhaps even this is an indication of her being more optimistic than her sisters, since she is the most inclined to think that simply being at home will bring her happiness.

LOVE AND LONELINESS

In many poets one would regard love and loneliness as separate themes, but in the Brontës they are inseparable. None of the Brontës experienced happiness in love – unless perhaps Charlotte very late in life, and after the period during which the poems in the Everyman collection were composed. Charlotte regarded herself as too plain for a man to be interested in her, but she continued to long for love. This almost certainly lies behind her lines in 'The Teacher's Monologue':

> Life will be gone ere I have lived;
> Where now is Life's first prime? (79–80)

Her poem 'He saw my heart's woe' is the bitter record of her disappointment in love, and her attempt to resign herself to a lonely life.

None of Anne's poems refers to a specific disappointment, although 'Dreams' and 'If This Be All' express her longing for love and motherhood. Branwell, on the other hand, wrote one of his most striking poems on the subject of disappointed love – 'Penmaenmawr'. Although his emotional resources for coping with his plight seem scant, he does not suggest that he feels doomed to a life of loneliness in the way that Charlotte does.

Emily was the most private of the Brontë siblings, and where love appears in her poems it does so through an assumed Gondal persona, and in the form of violent attraction and irreconcilable opposites. Like *Wuthering Heights*, these poems seem to deal with emotional archetypes rather than real people. Thus we find the bitter suicidal passion of 'F. De Samara to A. G. A.', the 'divinest anguish' (31) of the speaker in 'Remembrance', the yearning of 'If grief for grief can touch thee', but also the gentle romantic appeal of 'Song by Julius Brenzaida to G. S.' Emily's treatment of love in most of these poems is very much in accord with *Wuthering Heights*, whose heroine Cathy, speaking of her feelings for Heathcliff, says:

If all else perished, and he remained, I should still continue to be; and if all else remained, and he were annihilated, the universe would turn to a mighty stranger: I should not seem a part of it. — My love for Linton is like the foliage in the woods: time will change it, I'm well aware, as winter changes the trees. My love for Heathcliff resembles the eternal rocks beneath: a source of little visible delight, but necessary. (Ch. 9)

Friendship, as a relative of love, appears in some of the poems in the selection. In Emily's 'Song' ('O between distress and pleasure') it is scornfully dismissed as a poor substitute for passion, but in 'Love is like the wild rose briar', she favours friendship over love, saying that, like the holly tree, it will remain vigorous after the rose of love has wilted away. Anne hints in 'If This Be All' that friendship alone is not enough for her. Only Branwell, in 'The man who will not know another', refers to a particular friendship – his relationship with Francis Grundy. In this poem, Branwell presents friendship as something of value, chastising Grundy for not showing it sufficiently, and recommending his own 'noble sympathies' (24).

NATURE

None of the Brontës focuses intimately on nature in the way that their contemporary John Clare does, but the natural world is nonetheless an inspiration to Emily and Anne in many of their poems, and a comfort to Branwell. In 'Penmaenmawr' he identifies with the rocky crag and wishes for its powers of endurance. It also embodies for him the 'sublimity' (4) of nature – a power which to some extent takes him out of himself by virtue of its indifference to human concerns. Anne's response to nature is sometimes one of pure joy, as in 'Lines Composed in a Wood on a Windy Day'. This poem's vigorous diction and metre echo the roaring wind, dancing leaves, scudding clouds and lashing sea that she describes, as well as her elation on being out on such a day:

CONTEXT

The image of Emily as a very private person is borne out by Charlotte's report that she was distressed by Charlotte discovering and reading her poems. Nonetheless, Emily agreed to their publication.

CHECK THE POEM

John Clare (1793–1864) wrote many poems which delight in nature for its own sake, rather than as an inspiration for ideas, as is often the case with the Brontës. They describe the woods or moors, but he focuses more closely, as in 'The Nightingale's Nest': 'Her wings would tremble in her ecstasy/ And feathers stand on end as twere with joy/ And mouth wide open to release her heart.' See *John Clare* (Everyman's Poetry, 1997).

> My soul is awakened, my spirit is soaring
> And carried aloft on the wings of the breeze;
> For above and around me the wild wind is roaring,
> Arousing the rapture the earth and the seas. (1–4)

'The Bluebell' expresses a similar delight, but here the initial observations lead on to sadder thoughts of lost childhood. 'Memory' is another poem full of simple joy in nature – and especially in flowers, but here nature inspires Anne to consider how we should interpret our memories of childhood.

Emily is often said to take a great delight in nature. However, even more than in the case of Anne, nature for Emily is an inspiration to her thoughts, and to her emotional response to the universe as a whole. Two stanzas from 'Loud without the wind was roaring' will demonstrate her great enjoyment of nature:

> For the moors, for the moors where the short grass
> Like velvet beneath us should lie!
> For the moors, for the moors, where each high pass
> Rose sunny against the clear sky!

> For the moors, where the linnet was trilling
> Its song on the old granite stone –
> Where the lark – the wild sky-lark was filling
> Every breast with delight like its own.

The repeated exclamations, the sensual details of 'short grass/ Like velvet' and 'the linnet … trilling' on the 'old granite stone', and the simple word 'delight' combine to create a great sense of positive energy. However, this is immediately contrasted with Emily's feelings 'in exile afar'. The poem which follows in the Everyman edition, 'The blue bell is the sweetest flower', expresses a similar mixture of emotion, with nature being both a source of delight and a spur to sadness. This poem does, however, contain a striking image expressing Emily's reverence for the natural world:

> The buds hid like a sapphire gem
> In sheaths of emerald hue. (31–2)

CHECK THE POEM
Skylarks have often been an inspiration to poets, especially **Romantic** ones. One famous example is Shelley's 'To a Skylark', which begins: 'Hail to thee, blithe spirit!/ Bird thou never wert,/ That from heaven, or near it,/ Pourest thy full heart/ In profuse strains of unpremeditated art.'

At other times, Emily projects her thoughts and feelings on to nature, as in 'The Night-Wind', in which the wind takes on the role of a male seducer, inviting her to join him in the woods. In 'Stars', she seems to be surprisingly ambivalent about nature, as if she has to forgo its daylight joys in order to experience the mystical union with the infinite that she associates with night.

There is in Emily and Anne something of the sense of the sublime in nature already mentioned in relation to Branwell (see **Detailed summaries: Penmaenmawr**). While Branwell perhaps finds some comfort in being dwarfed by the massive structure of Penmaenmawr, Emily finds an almost perverse pleasure in the bleakness of nature in winter. It is as if the seasonal inevitability of the time when 'ice upon the glancing stream/ Has cast its sombre shade' ('The blue bell is the sweetest flower', 13–14) inspires her with a grandeur that transcends humanity. At an emotional level, too, winter strikes a chord with the inner bleakness that she feels at least some of the time. One finds this, too, in *Wuthering Heights*. Lockwood, for example, at the start of Chapter 2, describes Wuthering Heights itself in typical terms: 'On that bleak hill-top the earth was hard with a black frost, and the air made me shiver through every limb.' Of the three, Anne takes the simplest pleasure in nature as a path to the sublime, as when she calls her '... willing soul away/ From earth, and air, and sky' ('Memory', 11–12) to imagine a primrose. While she is not averse to wild weather, she lacks Emily's special attraction to it.

IMAGINATION

Poets are naturally concerned with imagination, but not many write about it in their poems. The Brontës, however, following in the Romantic tradition, were interested enough in it to write several poems featuring this theme. Perhaps for them, imagination played a special role. The Brontë myth, for which Mrs Gaskell's biography of Charlotte is largely responsible, has it that the Brontës lived extremely isolated lives. This has led some critics to write about the special importance of imagination in their lives. However, it is more likely that their closeness as children contributed more to this, as they collaborated in developing shared fantasy worlds, feeding off each other's ideas. In the case

CHECK THE BOOK

In his *Biographia Literaria*, the **Romantic** poet Samuel Taylor Coleridge writes: 'The primary Imagination I hold to be the living power and prime agent of all human perception, and as a repetition in the finite mind of the eternal act of creation in the infinite I AM.'

of the three sisters, however, the limitations forced upon women in Victorian times may also have encouraged them to find fulfilment in imagination.

Charlotte's 'Retrospection' describes the world of fantasy that she and her sisters and brother wove as children. Appropriately, she uses four images: a web, a spring, a mustard seed and an almond rod. In adulthood, each image has grown to vast proportions. Branwell speaks ambivalently about imagination in 'Death Triumphant', seeming to be comforted yet confused by it. Anne also expresses a certain ambivalence in 'Dreams', in which she begins by taking comfort in her ability to daydream about love and motherhood, only to plunge back into 'the dreary void' (24) on coming back to reality. Only Emily fully embraces the imaginative faculty, and her poem 'To Imagination' carefully explains her relationship with it. She realises well enough the difference between the imagined and the real: 'I trust not to thy phantom bliss' (31). Yet it seems to be her very acceptance of this distinction that enables her to experience imagination as a separate reality, and one which can facilitate mystical experience. Imagination for her is a 'Benignant Power' (34) that has the ability 'to bring/ The hovering vision back' (26). It is far from being merely a source of mental escapism.

SPIRITUAL YEARNING

It is not surprising that the children of a clergyman, brought up in a parsonage overlooking a graveyard, should be concerned with religion. One might think, too, that having lost their mother and two sisters, they would seek spiritual comfort and contemplate the nature of the afterlife. However, the Brontës all seem to yearn for something more fulfilling than this earthly life, as if mourning a lost Eden, an ideal pre-birth state of oneness with the universe. They share with Wordsworth a kind of divine homesickness, which he famously expressed in his 'Intimations of Immortality from Recollections of Early Childhood':

> Our birth is but a sleep and a forgetting:
> The Soul that rises with us, our life's Star,
> Hath had elsewhere its setting,
> And cometh from afar:

CONTEXT

The belief that when we are born into this world we come with some faint memory of an ideal realm, to which we yearn to return, is thought to have been originally propounded by Plato (427–347 BCE).

Not in entire forgetfulness,
And not in utter nakedness,
But trailing clouds of glory do we come
From God, who is our home:
Heaven lies about us in our infancy!

Yet, despite their shared upbringing, and their influence on each other, each of them expresses this yearning in a particular form. Charlotte's is the most conventional. It seems at times as if her real yearning is for love, and that this is merely channelled into religious feelings because of her chronic loneliness. In 'He saw my heart's woe' this process is made explicit. She speaks of the man she loves, and who fails to love her in return, as a stone idol, a 'Granite God [who] had felt no tenderness' (15). Regretting what she now sees as her folly, she turns with more bitterness than joy to the 'King eternal' (23), from human love denied, to the love of God. A similar overlapping of romantic and spiritual yearning can perhaps be seen in Anne's 'The Captive Dove', in which she portrays the dove – a symbol of spirit – as yearning for freedom. At the same time, it would be happier in its captive (earth-bound) state if it only had a mate.

Branwell declared himself an atheist, to the disappointment of his father and his sister Anne, who was also distressed by his dismissal from Thorp Green, where she worked as well. Her distress was almost certainly caused by her anxiety for his soul in the light of his affair with his employer's wife. His own letters of the time betray no such religious anxieties. Nonetheless, some of his later poems suggest that he either regained his faith or at least adopted some degree of faith as a conventional stance. His 'Oh Thou, whose beams were most withdrawn' and 'O God! while I in pleasure's wiles' lack Anne's religious fervour but do represent a degree of spiritual seeking, albeit cloaked in Branwell's characteristic tendency to dramatise his own situation and feelings. In the former, Branwell perceives God as frowning on him, and asks for 'one short space of rest' (15) before death, and in the latter he asks for 'the stern sustaining power' (5) to face death when it comes.

Anne is the most passionate in her Christianity. Several poems in this selection speak of her religious doubts and self-recrimination, as

> **CONTEXT**
>
> The dove was a popular symbol of spiritual liberation in Victorian times. The German composer Felix Mendelssohn wrote a hymn in 1844, with a famous passage known as 'O for the wings of a dove'. It contains the lines, 'O for the wings, for the wings of a dove!/ Far away, far away would I rove!/ In the wilderness build me a nest,/ and remain there forever at rest.'

well as her occasional rejoicing. In 'Despondency' she describes what is sometimes termed a 'dark night of the soul', in which she cannot find any sense of connection with God. The poem which follows after it, however, 'In Memory of a Happy Day in February', expresses just the opposite: a jubilant assertion of her absolute faith in redemption. It is particularly striking in the light of her struggle with Calvinism, which had made her doubt that she would ever achieve heaven (see the **Detailed summary** on this poem). Her 'Last Lines' shows great faith, and a determination to serve God to the end of her life.

Emily's spirituality is really in a class of its own. She is far from conventionally Christian, notably rejecting in 'No coward soul is mine' the 'thousand creeds/ That move men's hearts'. To her, they are:

> … unutterably vain,
> Worthless as withered weeds
> Or idlest froth amid the boundless main. (10–12)

Here as elsewhere, for example in 'Tell me, tell me, smiling child', her image of the boundless ocean represents her vision of the infinite. Time and again she seeks to breach the limits of earthly life. In 'The Prisoner' and 'To A Wreath of Snow, by A. G. Almeda' the earthly form is symbolised by physical imprisonment. Light, or snow, filtering down through a distant grill represents a hope of spiritual escape. At the same time, earth itself is terribly important in her poems, as a bedrock of life, and is therefore often mentioned – for example, in 'Remembrance'. The physical body must return to earth in order for the natural world to continue its eternal round, and for the individual spirit to merge with the infinite. Thus in 'Death', speaking both of Time and her own life, she insists –

> Strike it down, that other boughs may flourish
> Where that perished sapling used to be;
> Thus, at least, its mouldering corpse will nourish
> That from which it sprung – Eternity. (29–33)

QUESTION

How would you summarise the differences between Emily's attitude towards religion and Anne's? You might try comparing 'No coward soul is mine' with 'In Memory of a Happy Day in February'.

STRUCTURE

The structure of the Everyman edition of the Brontës' poems is straightforward. The four siblings are in order of age, with Charlotte, the eldest, coming first, and Anne, the youngest, last. Within these sections, the poems are arranged chronologically, so we can sometimes see a progression of ideas. Thus, Anne's 'If this be all' is very similar in theme to 'Dreams', and a glance at the notes (at the back of the Everyman edition) reveals that it was written soon afterwards. Of course, the editor has made a personal selection, so we cannot be sure that no poems were written in between those included. In many cases, moreover, we cannot be sure exactly when a poem was composed. The selection includes a cross-section of poems, for example Emily's Gondal and non-Gondal poems. Charlotte's narrative poems are represented only by 'Mementos', perhaps because she writes more effectively as a poet in more intimate forms, rather than in a narrative style, which she handles better in her novels.

LANGUAGE AND STYLE

IMAGERY AND ALLUSION

Just as one can identify themes that are common to all of the Brontës, but which they deal with in their individually characteristic ways, so one can with their use of imagery and other poetic techniques. This section identifies techniques and types of imagery used by the Brontës, along with the personal tendencies of each sibling.

Personification

In common with many **Victorian** poets, all of the Brontës use personification at times. The appeal of this technique is that it can enable abstract concepts and qualities such as liberty, memory, faith or death to be discussed in a less abstract way by giving them the characteristics of living things. However, the technique can produce very dry verse, with little appeal to the senses, and, even when used well, it is best used in moderation. Among the Brontës, Anne uses personification least, because she has least need for it, writing more

CHECK THE BOOK

It should be borne in mind that all four siblings wrote poems other than those included in the Everyman collection. *The Selected Poems* edited by Stevie Smith, for example, includes some good poems, especially by Emily, not included in the Everyman selection. See, for example, Emily's 'I'll come when thou art saddest'. There are also separate collected editions of poems by all three sisters.

CONTEXT

Use of **personification** in English poetry goes back at least to Geoffrey Chaucer (1343–1400), who uses it in *The Canterbury Tales*. In *The Pardoner's Tale* he personifies Death as a thief.

CONTEXT

Anne's image of the buttercup as a 'goblet' suggests a fairy's golden cup. In **Victorian** times there was still a widespread folk belief in fairies. Poets and artists were fascinated by the idea of fairies. See, for example, the long poem *Goblin Market* by Christina Rossetti (1830–94), and the painting 'The Fairy Feller's Master Stroke', by Richard Dadd (1817–86).

CHECK THE BOOK

Charlotte's appeal to Reason, Patience and Faith echoes *The Pilgrim's Progress* by John Bunyan (1628–88), a Christian **allegory** which was still influential in Victorian times and would have been familiar to Charlotte. It includes such characters as Discretion, Prudence, Piety and Charity.

about the natural world and her own feelings than about abstractions. Her use of personification is usually barely noticeable, and its effect is vaguely pleasant rather than striking. In 'The Bluebell' she writes of 'smiling flowers' (15), in 'In Memory of a Happy Day in February' the 'smile of early spring' (9), and in 'Home' 'That sun surveys a lovely scene/ From softly smiling skies' (5–6). Only in 'Memory' does she use personification more fully, and her use of the technique is effective because she fleshes out her address to Memory with natural details that appeal strongly to the senses, as well as enlivening these with some additional imagery. For example:

Still in the wall-flower's fragrance dwell;
And hover round the slight blue bell,
My childhood's darling flower.
Smile on the little daisy still,
The buttercup's bright goblet fill
With all thy former power.   (lines 25–30)

Her request that Memory should 'dwell' in the fragrance of the wall-flower is delicately worded. The personal note of 'My childhood's darling flower' is appealing, and the metaphor of the buttercup's 'bright goblet' is fresh and effective.

Charlotte's use of personification is often less successful. In 'The Teacher's Monologue', for example, her identification of 'Joy and transient Sorrow' (37) as the sun and rain that have ripened her hopes is rather laboured. Elsewhere in the poem she tends to overuse the technique, peopling it with seven personified abstractions: 'Patience, weary with her yoke' (75), 'Health's elastic spring' (77), 'Death/ A welcome, wished-for friend;/ Then, aid me, Reason, Patience, Faith...' (87–9). The phrases describing Patience and Health are rather conventional, while her use of Fate in the final stanza of 'Parting' is less enlivened than it might be. However, 'The Autumn day its course has run' is a different matter altogether. Here, Charlotte is personifying Twilight rather than something more conceptual, and is focusing on one idea. Most of this short poem develops this personification in an atmospheric and arresting way, with Twilight being named first as 'a silent guest' (3), and then as 'silent Nun' (7).

Branwell makes some use of personification, especially relating to memory. Thus, the opening stanza of the poem 'Memory' is not strikingly original in concept, but is effectively worded nonetheless. He describes the 'magic fingers' of memory, which 'Wake the chord whose spirit lingers' (1–3). In 'The man who will not know another', he briefly describes Nature as spurning the man who shuns another. In 'Death Triumphant', he personifies the Self and the Soul, the latter more extensively. However, the most subtle user of personification of the four siblings is Emily. An example of her subtlety is 'Alone I sat', in which she speaks of a 'solemn joy around me stealing' (9). The idea of 'solemn joy' is itself unusual and exciting, but the image of it 'stealing' – creeping up on her stealthily – is even more so.

At other times, Emily uses personification much more extensively – not by cramming several examples into one poem, but by building a single personification into a profound symbol. She does this, for example, in 'To A Wreath of Snow, by A. G. Almeda', in which the snow, beautifully addressed as 'transient voyager of heaven!'(1), is a symbol of awakening and sustaining spirit. Emily uses the technique in this extended way in a number of other poems. In 'The Night-Wind', the wind itself could be described as a personification, but of something unusually elusive – perhaps the seductiveness of the sensual world. In 'Hope', she personifies her own experience of hope as a friend who is, paradoxically, timid but cruel. In the space of a few stanzas, this 'friend' is brought to life both as a character and an emotional concept . Emily's 'To Imagination' risks overusing personification by introducing too many concepts – Imagination, Liberty, Reason, Nature, Truth and Fancy. Nonetheless, she brings them to life by showing them in relationship with each other, and with just enough lifelike detail. For example, we see Truth 'rudely' trampling 'The flowers of Fancy, newly-blown' (23–4). Emily's most striking use of the technique, however, is surely 'Stars', in which she powerfully personifies daylight, through the sun, as a violent, penetrating male figure invading her bedroom.

> **CONTEXT**
>
> **Romantic** poet Shelley uses personification in 'The Masque of Anarchy' to satirise contemporary Establishment figures. He begins: 'I met Murder on the way –/ He had a mask like Castlereagh.' Castlereagh was Foreign Secretary in 1819, and disliked by radicals for his right-wing politics and his support for the suppression of dissent.

> **CONTEXT**
>
> Most cultures perceive the sun as masculine and the moon as feminine. Emily's image of the sun might be compared with a Navajo Indian myth in which a young woman, lying on a rock to dry herself after bathing, is penetrated and impregnated by the sun, in the form of a sunbeam.

Nature, weather and the seasons

All four Brontës make use of the weather and the seasons in their poems, either in imagery or in settings. Charlotte uses these, and nature imagery in general, the least, essentially because she was far less of an 'outdoor type' than her sisters. Where her poems have settings, they tend to be indoors, as in 'Mementos', which is set in a big old gothic house. When she uses images from nature, they have the ring of formality, as if taken from literature rather than personal observation. In 'Retrospection', for example, her metaphors for childhood imagination – the web, the spring, the mustard seed and the almond rod – are interesting but hardly lifelike. The mustard seed and the almond rod are biblical (see the **Detailed summary** on the poem), the spring is a commonplace symbol of inspiration, and the 'web of sunny air' (2), with folds which turn crimson, 'ruby-red' (19), is unusual, but does not relate to anything actually found in nature. Her spring's 'feeble roar' (2) lacks all verisimilitude. In 'The Teacher's Monologue' she presents her hopes, cherished by the 'sun and rain' (36) of the **personified** Joy and Sorrow, ripening to a harvest of 'golden sheaves' which she now fears are merely 'empty air' (40). This is conventional Christian imagery of the hymn-book variety. Her reference to 'The bitter blasts that blight the heart' ('Mementos', 208), her assertion that God will 'Wash out with dews of bliss the fiery brand of woe' ('He saw my heart's woe', 28), and her portrayal of herself as 'benighted, tempest-tossed' ('On the death of Anne Brontë', 15) are vigorous but conventional.

Branwell's use of nature imagery is surprisingly lacking in aptness or originality, considering that he enjoyed walking and therefore saw nature at first-hand rather more than Charlotte did. In 'Augusta' he personifies the moon as a marching woman, and describes the clouds as having 'whitened fleeces'. At other times he describes his own troubles in terms of cloudy skies and storms, as in 'Oh Thou, whose beams were most withdrawn', 'Lines Written at Thorp Green', and 'Epistle From a Father to a Child in Her Grave'. His use of natural settings for his poems is more interesting. For example, in 'Death Triumphant', his evocation of the 'bright Mayday morn' and his appeal for his 'bitter thoughts' to be carried away 'With the wild winter it has driven!' (1–4) does have the ring of truth. His 'Penmaenmawr', too, makes effective use of the central

CHECK THE BOOK
The house in 'Mementos' is rather like Rochester's in *Jane Eyre*. Both seem to hide secrets from the past.

CHECK THE BOOK
The Brontës' use of the seasons, and especially Branwell's rather formal use of them in 'Death Triumphant', reminds one of the opening to Shakespeare's *Richard III*: 'Now is the winter of our discontent/ Made glorious summer by this sun of York.'

image of the storm-battered rugged outcrop gazing out over a restless sea.

Anne's use of nature in settings and imagery is unaffected and appealing. Occasionally a lapse into the conventional reminds us of Charlotte:

> If clouds must ever keep from sight
>   The glories of the Sun,
> And I must suffer Winter's blight,
>   Ere Summer is begun. ('If This Be All', 25–8)

At other times, her imagery is low-key but fairly effective. In 'Lines Written at Thorp Green' she writes of the wind's 'icy dart' (10) and the 'rustling music' (17) of the leaves, in 'Home' of the 'velvet lawns' of Thorp Green, and in 'The Consolation' of 'ice that gathers round my heart' (24). She uses nature most effectively, however, as an inspiration. In 'The Bluebell' she is moved by the 'silent eloquence' of 'every wild bluebell' (5–6), in 'Lines Written at Thorp Green' she employs the seasons as indicators of the time that must pass before she can go home. In other poems, such as 'Memory' and 'Lines Composed in a Wood on a Windy Day', she simply rejoices in nature.

It is Emily who makes the most effective and original use of nature, both in terms of **imagery** and in her settings. Many of her images are unremarkable in their basic conception, but turned into something original and evocative by the way in which she refines them. In 'Tell me, tell me, smiling child', for example, her image of the past as 'An Autumn evening soft and mild' is given an extra depth by its 'wind that sights mournfully' (3–4). The 'green and flowery spray' of the present is deepened by the added detail of the fledgling bird sitting on it and 'gathering its power/ To mount and fly away' (7–8). In 'To a Wreath of Snow, by A. G. Almeda', her image of morning rising is enriched by the double sense of 'When morning rose in mourning grey' (15). At times, she conjures up an arresting imagery for natural phenomena, as in 'The blue bell is the sweetest flower':

<aside>
CONTEXT

The sensual details that one finds in many of Emily's poems may seem at odds with her spirituality, but she apparently enjoyed doing down-to-earth household chores.
</aside>

> The heavens have lost their zone of gold,
> The earth its robe of green.
>
> … ice upon the glancing stream   (11–13)
>
> The buds hid like a sapphire gem
> In sheaths of emerald hue.   (31–2)

Here, as in a number of her poems, part of the charm lies in the appeal to the senses, which makes her chosen details spring to life. At times these are visual, as in 'darker waves round the long heather' (25), in 'Loud without the wind was roaring', at others aural or even musical, as in lines 47–8 of this poem: 'the linnet was trilling/ Its song on the old granite stone'.

Two special sorts of nature imagery are commonly used by Emily. The first is the sea, as an image of the infinite, or the indefinable space that the soul must cross between life and death. In 'Tell me, tell me, smiling child', the child perceives the future as:

> A sea beneath a cloudless sun,
> A mighty glorious dazzling sea
> Stretching into infinity.   (10–12)

In 'Song ("O between distress and pleasure")' the speaker attempts to conjure up a hopeful future, with infinite possibilities, declaring that he will become 'an Ocean rover' sailing 'the desert sea' (11–12). On the other hand, in 'A Death-Scene', death is 'the eternal sea'. Most strikingly, in 'No coward soul is mine', Emily portrays the world's religions as 'Worthless as withered weeds/ Or idlest froth amid the boundless main' (11–12). Paradoxically, she holds fast to the infinity of her inner God; she is 'anchored on/ The steadfast rock of Immortality' (15–16).

Emily's image of 'withered weeds' is also an example of her second common use of nature imagery – that which springs from the plant world. One outstanding example is 'Love is like the wild rose briar', in which love and friendship are likened to the rose and the holly. A more complex example is found in 'Death'. The poet identifies with

---

CONTEXT

Although Emily uses the sea **metaphorically**, it was Anne who had a special love of the real sea. When she knew she was dying, she asked to be taken on a last holiday to Scarborough, where she died and is buried.

QUESTION

How do you think Emily's extended **metaphor** in 'Death' compares with Charlotte's extended metaphor for childhood inspiration in 'Retrospection'?

Time, picturing herself, and time itself, as a 'withered branch' springing from Eternity. Being human, she is 'withered', while Eternity remains 'fresh' (3). She develops this metaphor over several stanzas.

Emily also uses nature extensively in the settings of her poems, especially in those which spring from the Gondal narrative. 'Remembrance' makes deeply symbolic and atmospheric use of setting. The repeated 'Cold in the earth' (1, 9) couples the earth, as our bedrock and physical destination, with the coldness of being beyond comfort. The snow is both bleak and chilling, but it also symbolises the purity of the speaker's devotion. We also see Emily's use of the seasons as an indicator of passing time: 'Fifteen wild Decembers...' (9). Both 'Song by Julius Brenzaida to G. S.' and 'F. De Samara to A. G. A.' also use weather and setting to evoke atmosphere. In the former, the ancient thorn tree perhaps symbolises the lovers' relationship, while in the latter, the 'northwind's bitter sigh' and 'rainy sky' (3–4) and the deserted moor and the 'tempest in the air' (9) perfectly evoke the speaker's mood.

Music

The Brontës were a musical family, and they all use musical imagery at times. Emily was the most talented musician of the family, and, unsurprisingly, her poems make the most use of such imagery. Comparisons of poetry with music are fairly common in nineteenth-century verse, so one should not regard this sort of imagery as exceptional. Keats, for example, pleads in his 'Ode to Psyche':

> So let me be thy choir, and make a moan
>   Upon the midnight hours;
> Thy voice, thy lute, thy pipe ...

Anne, favouring simplicity, rarely uses this sort of image. The phrase 'rustling music' in 'Lines Written at Thorp Green' is one example. Charlotte uses musical imagery conventionally, for example in 'The Teacher's Monologue':

CHECK THE POEM
'A. E. and R. C.', written around the same time as 'Remembrance' (spring of 1845), uses repetition of key words to create a powerful emotional mood. In 'A. E. and R. C.', **'heavy'** is used five times in the opening eight lines – four of those at the start of a line, where it has particular force, as with the use of **'Cold'** in 'Remembrance'.

CONTEXT

A contemporary reviewer of the Brontë sisters' *Poems* (1846) noted the musicality of the verse, adding that Ellis Bell (Emily's pseudonym) displayed this quality more than the other two poets.

CHECK THE POEM

Tennyson uses musical **imagery** in 'The Lotos-Eaters'; for example: 'Music that gentlier on the spirit lies,/ Than tired eyelids upon tired eyes.'

CONTEXT

Shelley, in his essay *A Defence of Poetry* (1820), relates poetry to music: 'Man is an instrument over which a series of external and internal impressions are driven, like the alternations of an ever-changing wind over an Aeolian lyre; which move it, by their motion, to ever-changing melody.'

> Tis not the air I wished to play,
> The strain I wished to sing;
> My wilful spirit slipped away
> And struck another string.   (51–4)

Charlotte favours extended **metaphors**, and she prolongs this one – but much in the same vein. Branwell's use of musical imagery is similar, though at times a little more original. In 'Memory', for example, he writes of Memory's 'magic fingers', which 'With a wild and passing thrill/ Wake the chord whose spirit lingers,/ Sleeping silently and still' (1–4). This mixture of **personification** and ordinary metaphor evokes the elusive power of memory and makes an effective opening to the poem. When Emily uses images of music, she makes more of them. For example, music is the starting point for 'Come hither, child', when the first speaker asks where the child acquired the 'power to touch that string so well' (2). As the child recounts its story, the music reaches mystical status, becoming 'a note … So full of soul, so deeply sweet' (25–6) that it makes the child think of Gabriel's trumpet announcing Judgement Day. In 'The Night-Wind', the wind is a 'gentle singer' (17), and, most memorably, in 'The Prisoner', the prisoner says that as the transcendental moment approaches, 'Mute music soothes my breast,/ unuttered harmony/ That I could never dream till earth was lost to me' (47–8). Musical imagery, then, comes naturally to all of the Brontës when they write of feeling and inspiration. Moreover, it is particularly appropriate to their verse, since it is largely led by emotion rather than intellect.

OTHER POETIC FEATURES

In the example above, the phrase 'Mute music' demonstrates a special feature of Emily's poetry, her surprising use of **oxymorons** that express the paradoxical truths and experiences which she is trying to communicate. In this phrase, the paradox is exaggerated by the **alliteration**, which seems to imply a similarity between the two words, although in everyday experience they are mutually exclusive. The poem further evokes the nature of the mystical experience in the phrases 'tender fire' and 'kill me with desire' (39–40). Other examples of this oxymoronic technique are found in 'Remembrance', in which the **narrator** speaks of 'memory's rapturous pain' and of 'divinest anguish' (30–31), expressing the extreme bitter-sweetness of such memory.

Closely related to **imagery**, though actually a **rhetorical device**, is synecdoche – the technique of referring to a whole by a representative part. Branwell uses this the most, perhaps because it is a classical technique, and he has the greatest tendency to echo the classics. One example is in 'The man who will not know another': 'His frozen eye, his bloodless heart,/ Nature, repugnant, bids depart' (5–6). He also uses it in 'Death Triumphant': 'Have I the footsteps bounding free,/ The happy laugh of infancy' (32–3). This second use is perhaps more effective, as it uses more appealing descriptive details than the first. Emily uses the technique occasionally, as in 'To a Wreath of Snow, by A. G. Almeda':

> Methinks the hands that shut the sun
> So sternly from this mourning brow
> Might still their rebel task have done.   (5–7)

Fictional voices

It is important to remember that the poems in the selection cannot be assumed to embody the poet's own attitudes and feelings in a straightforward way. Each of the Brontës writes, at times, from the viewpoint of a **persona**. This relates, of course, to the fact that all four had grown up writing stories about the fictional characters of the Angria and Gondal stories, and some of Emily's best poems emerged from this background. Much of Anne's best poetry is intimate and even confessional, and so she uses literary voices the least – and in the Everyman selection not at all. All three sisters were novelists, and so they were accustomed to expressing views and feelings not entirely their own through their characters. There are many poems in the selection, of course, which one can safely regard as expressing, direct and unmasked, the poet's own sentiments. Obvious examples are Charlotte's 'The Teacher's Monologue', as well as the poems on the deaths of her sisters.

Charlotte wrote **narrative** poems using assumed voices, but it is generally thought that these are not among her best. She expresses character much better in the medium of the novel. The only clear

CHECK THE BOOK
Branwell was well-versed in the classics, and he may have come across the phrase 'his frozen eye' in *Cupid and Psyche: A Mythological Tale, from the 'Golden Ass' of Apuleius.* Translated by Hudson Gurney and originally published in 1800, it was republished in 1842. It contains these lines: 'He does not wring his aged hands –/ No tear-drop fills his frozen eye.'

CHECK THE POEM
One use of narrative voice, and indeed poetic **framed narrative**, with which the Brontës would undoubtedly have been familiar, is Samuel Taylor Coleridge's *The Rime of the Ancient Mariner*, published in 1798.

example of her using a fictional voice in the Everyman selection is 'Mementos', which one can imagine being spoken by an aged and sympathetic housekeeper who has observed the goings-on of the household over many years and now reports them. 'Early wrapt in slumber deep' may have a **narrative** context, but no attempt is made to give the speaker a personality. Branwell uses narrative voices, but without developing character very much. His 'Augusta' assumes the voice of an Angrian character lovingly addressing his wife – not something Branwell could write about from personal experience. 'On Caroline' assumes the persona, but one closely allied to Branwell himself. In his translation 'To Sestius' he takes on the voice of Horace. His most striking use of an assumed **persona** of his own is probably 'Now – but one moment, let me stay', in which he succeeds in giving a real sense of a speaker poised on the brink of war, enjoying a moment of calm before risking his life.

Emily's 'No coward soul is mine', too, is clearly a statement of her personal creed. However, her Gondal poems, in which she speaks through a persona, contain no less depth of feeling. In 'Remembrance', for example, she was able to apply her own very real sense of loss to a fictional scenario. In a mystical poem such as 'To a Wreath of Snow, by A. G. Almeda', she was able to express her own experience in the context of an imaginary prisoner. Where she often succeeds in the use of a narrative voice more than her siblings is in her characterisation. In 'To a Wreath of Snow, by A. G. Almeda', we learn that the speaker is 'a mountaineer,/ Who, all life long has loved the snow' (21–2). In 'F. De Samara to A. G. A.' we find the deeply divided feelings of a speaker who loves a woman enough to kill himself because he is losing her, but who nonetheless longs to give her pain in return: 'Oh could I know thy soul with equal grief was torn –/ This fate might be endured' (27–8). In 'Remembrance' we find a very different character, who is bitterly determined to live, despite her loss.

One special feature of some of Emily's Gondal poems, shared by some of Anne's (though not in this selection), is the use of internal dialogue, a technique which enables the poet to create a dynamic juxtaposition of ideas by using two speakers. 'Tell me, tell me, smiling child' is one example, where an adult asks questions and

the child reveals a vision of the past, present and future. 'To
A. G. A.' is another example – one in which our curiosity is
aroused by the questioner. 'Come hither, child' and 'The Prisoner'
are special examples, since the dialogue takes place within a
framed narrative.

Diction

All the Brontës have a tendency towards using certain sorts of
language. In commenting on their **diction**, or word choice, critics
have pointed out that their vocabulary is repetitive, and this is
certainly true. It is based to some extent on their themes and
outlook on life. Thus we find the frequent occurrence of words
relating to life generally being rather depressing. Charlotte dwells
on her own loneliness and on life having to be endured. Her mood
in 'On the Death of Emily Jane Brontë' is, of course,
understandably grim, but its language is still only an exaggeration of
that which occurs in her other poems. Looking out on 'life's lone
wilderness', she questions:

'Weary, weary, dark and drear,
How shall I the burden bear
   The burden and distress?'   (15–18)

The words 'weary', 'dark', 'drear' (and 'dreary'), 'burden' and
'distress' occur frequently in many of the Brontës' poems, along
with words of similar emotional hue: 'anguish' (often conveniently
rhymed with 'languish'), 'agony', 'despair', 'despondency', and
'misery'. Branwell is slightly less inclined towards this sort of
language than Charlotte. Nonetheless, in 'Epistle From a Father to a
Child in Her Grave' he speaks of 'that drear country called "the
Life of Man"' (61), and of 'the borders of despair' (70). In
'Penmaenmawr', too, he speaks of his 'hopeless grief' (55) and
'despair' (80). More typically of him, he complains of life being full
of trouble and worry. In the final line of 'Epistle From a Father to a
Child in Her Grave', the child is 'freed from care!' (71). In
'Penmaenmawr' his heart is 'worn down by care' (10), and he
complains of 'ceaseless strife and change' (36), and of having to
weather 'affliction's storm' (62).

**CHECK
THE POEM**
A form of internal
dialogue is used by
Wordsworth in his
'The Leech-
Gatherer' (also
known as
'Resolution and
Independence'), in
which the poet
describes meeting
an aged leech-
gatherer and asking
him how he makes
his living.

**CHECK
THE POEM**
Tennyson's poem
'Mariana', published
in 1830, contains a
chorus similar to
some of the
Brontës' lines,
though more direct:
'She only said, "My
life is dreary,/ He
cometh not," she
said;/ She said, "I am
aweary, aweary,/ I
would that I were
dead!"'.

Many of Emily's poems contain this sort of repetitive language, with a special emphasis on the comfortless, unsheltered nature of life. This is sometimes supplied **symbolically** by the weather, as in the opening **stanza** of 'F. De Samara to A. G. A.':

> I'm drear and lone and far away –
> Cold blows on my breast, and northwind's bitter sigh
> And oh, my couch is bleak beneath the rainy sky! (2–4)

'The Prisoner', similarly, features 'gloom and desolate despair' (34), 'agony' (53) and 'anguish' (58), and the final stanza of 'Remembrance' rhymes 'languish' with 'anguish'. Emily is also fond of the word 'vain' to suggest the futility of human endeavour:

> Wretched hearts in vain would treasure ...
> ('Song ("O between distress and pleasure")', 3)

> Vain words – vain frenzied thoughts!
> ('F. De Samara to A. G. A.', 37)

> Vain are the thousand creeds
> That move men's hearts, unutterably vain ...
> ('No coward soul is mine', 9–10)

However, not quite all is doom and gloom in the world of the Brontës. Anne is generally more positive than the others in her **diction**. She speaks of 'anguish' and 'grief' in 'Despondency', but more often uses such words as 'bliss', 'blissful' and even 'merriment' (all in 'The Bluebell'). In 'In Memory of a Happy Day in February' we find 'rapture' and 'transient bliss', in 'Dreams' 'bliss' and 'raptures'. Elsewhere her words often convey a sense of softness, as in 'Home': 'Softly smiling skies' (6).

Emily, too, balances her mournful tones with language of transcendental joy. In 'Remembrance', the word 'bliss' is used in a negative sense, but it at least indicates that the speaker has experienced happiness in the past:

QUESTION

Do you feel that Emily Brontë was generally despairing, or is it the case that she is actually deeply hopeful in longing for a better life to come?

All my life's bliss from thy dear life was given,
All my life's bliss is in the grave with thee. (19–20)

Elsewhere Emily uses the language of joy in images of light. In 'To a
Wreath of Snow, by A. G. Almeda', we find: 'Thy silvery form so
soft and fair/ Shining through darkness, sweetly spoke' (18–19). In
'Stars', the sun is more ambivalently described. We find 'dazzling
sun/ Restored our Earth to joy' (1–2), but also 'hide me from the
hostile light' (43).

One other special feature of Emily's language is its use of words
relating to spirit. For example: 'eternity' ('Death'), 'eternal' ('A
Death-Scene'), 'Immortality' ('No coward soul is mine'), 'infinity'
('No coward soul is mine', 'Tell me, tell me, smiling child'). She also
favours words that suggest a blurring of perception, or of
movement between earthly and spiritual realms. Hence the snow in
the first line of 'To a Wreath of Snow, by A. G. Almeda' is
addressed as 'transient voyager of heaven' (1). In 'Alone I sat' we
find 'misty hill' (4) and, in 'A. E. and R. C.', 'Heavy broods the
damp mist' (3). In both, the mist casts a veil over everyday reality.

> **? QUESTION**
>
> How would you describe the tone of the Brontës' poems?

In addition to this tendency to make frequent use of certain words,
the Brontës also share a liking for what they regard as 'poetic
language'. Word order is often inverted, sometimes for the sake of a
rhyme, but sometimes because the poet seems to think that poetry
as a form demands it. At times, this can be very effective, as in
Charlotte's line in 'The Autumn day its course has run', 'And
Twilight to my lonely house a silent guest is come –' (3). She could
have written, 'And Twilight, a silent guest, has come to my lonely
house', but her actual line flows mellifluously and presents the ideas
in her preferred word order, while the form 'is come', rather than
'has come' draws the reader into an ongoing present moment, as if
time is somehow standing still. Moreover, the slight mystification
matches the sense. At other times the inversion seems awkward, as
in Branwell's line in 'To Sestius', 'Nor shun refitted ships the
silenced sea' (2). In addition, the Brontës, in common with most
other poets of the time use archaic words such as 'thou', 'thine' and
'thee', perhaps to elevate their poetry above the ordinariness of
everyday speech. Perhaps more significantly, they also commonly

avoid references to everyday things. Not one of their poems mentions eating or drinking in any realistic sense, nor any of the normal objects around the house. Nature can be discussed, but not furniture! One feature that makes Emily's 'Stars' appeal to a modern reader is its rare mention of realistic details; her pillow, the 'roof and floor' (34) and the curtains of her bedroom.

Rhythm and rhyme

Poetry in the early **Victorian** era was largely expected to rhyme and to have a **metre** of some sort. The Brontës were not great innovators in this respect, and their poems are generally fairly conventional in form. However, there is an art in choosing a fitting **metre** and rhyme scheme for the mood and subject. Moreover, the metre can be varied to produce a particular effect, and rhyme can be used to emphasise words – for example bringing two rhyming words into closer relationship with each other. An example of a well-chosen metre is Emily's 'Remembrance', in which the predominantly **dactylic** rhythm drags like a funeral march, or like the slow swell of a sea of contained emotion. In addition, there is a **caesura** near the middle of each line, which helps to slow the line down, producing the funereal effect, but which is also like a voice breaking with emotion, or which could suggest the separation of the lovers. The poem also makes highly effective use, in **stanza 5**, of repetition, an effect which would not be nearly so powerful in free verse. As for rhyme, it contains the rather obvious 'languish … anguish' (29–31) already mentioned, but also the cleverly contrasted 'perished … cherished' (21–3).

CHECK THE BOOK

The dactylic rhythm of 'Remembrance', with its caesura in each line, is similar to the commonest metrical form in Anglo-Saxon poetry such as *Beowulf*, which can be heard in a modern verse translation by poet Seamus Heaney (Faber, 1999). Heaney preserves the original metre.

Critics have suggested that the Brontës tended to regard poetic form as a ready-made mould into which they poured their ideas. If this is true, their poetry is often at its best metrically when it breaks the mould. Charlotte's 'Retrospection', for example, has an extra three lines in its fourth stanza, and a final line rhyming with its fourth line. These both suggest the sophistication of adulthood. Other examples of bold metrical variation are found in Emily's 'Alone I sat' (stanza 2) and 'Loud without the wind was roaring', in which the first and second stanzas, and the rest of the poem, are in three different metres. Another feature which helps to 'break the mould' is the avoidance of **end-stopped** lines, through **enjambment**.

Charlotte is sometimes guilty of writing metrical verse too rigidly, with end-stopped lines, as in the first three stanzas of 'Retrospection'. However, at times she uses enjambment with subtle sensitivity – for example in the opening two lines of 'The Teacher's Monologue' and, in the final stanza of 'Early wrapt in slumber deep'.

Rhythmically, Branwell strives for a certain grandeur, and he favours regular **heroic couplets**, as in 'Penmaenmawr' and 'Epistle From a Father to a Child in Her Grave'. However, he can vary his metre effectively, as in 'Now – but one moment, let me stay', which alternates short and long stanzas. Anne's verse is perhaps the most guilty of a lack of variation, but it still achieves a freshness through its simple but well-chosen words. The opening of 'Memory' is a good example. The placing of 'upon' at the end of the second line for the sake of rhyme is weak, and the rhythm is perfectly regular. Despite this, the overall effect is appealing because of the visual detail and the **alliteration**. The phrase 'waving woods' (2), for example, combines both of these, succinctly picturing the woods moving gently in the summer breeze.

> **? QUESTION**
> Do you find that the relative simplicity and regularity of Anne's verse makes it fresh and engaging, or rather bland?

PART FOUR

CRITICAL PERSPECTIVES

READING CRITICALLY

This section provides a range of critical viewpoints and perspectives on the poetry of the Brontës and gives a broad overview of key debates, interpretations and theories proposed since the poems were published. It is important to bear in mind the variety of interpretations and responses these poems have produced, many of them shaped by the critics' own backgrounds and historical contexts.

No single view of the poems should be seen as dominant – it is important that you arrive at your own judgements by questioning the perspectives described, and by developing your own critical insights. Objective analysis is a skill achieved through coupling close reading with an informed understanding of the key ideas, related texts and background information relevant to the text. These elements are all crucial in enabling you to assess the interpretations of other readers, and even to view works of criticism as texts in themselves. The ability to read critically will serve you well both in your study of the text, and in any critical writing, presentation, or further work you undertake.

EARLY RECEPTION

The very earliest responses to the Brontës' poetry were not encouraging. Branwell sent some verse to Wordsworth, together with a letter which managed to be both boastful and ingratiating – and received no reply. Charlotte sent some of her poems to the Poet Laureate Robert Southey in 1837, when she was twenty-one. She did receive a reply, but not an especially encouraging one. He wrote:

> You evidently possess, and in no inconsiderable degree, what Wordsworth calls the 'faculty of verse'. I am not depreciating it when I say that in these times it is not rare. Many volumes of

CONTEXT

In his letter to Wordsworth, Branwell called Wordsworth 'one whose works I have most loved in our Literature and who most has been with me a divinity of the mind'. He tactlessly added: 'Surely in this day when there is not a writing poet worth a sixpence the field must be open if a better man can step forward ...' Robert Southey noted that Wordsworth was 'disgusted' with the letter.

poems are now published every year without attracting public attention, any one of which, if it had appeared half a century ago, would have obtained a high reputation for its author. ...

... Literature cannot be the business of a woman's life, and it ought not to be. The more she is engaged in her proper duties, the less leisure will she have for it, even as an accomplishment and a recreation.

By 'proper duties' Southey refers to the activities middle and upper class **Victorian** women were expected to perform – either domestic tasks such as managing the home, or leisure activities such as painting and embroidery – which kept them separate from the public, and usually male-dominated, sphere of work. Charlotte was discouraged, but by 1845 had rallied sufficiently to persuade her sisters to join her in producing a volume of poetry. When this was published in 1846, it met with quite a favourable critical reception – despite selling only two copies! One critic praised their 'good, wholesome, refreshing, vigorous poetry'. Another noted, quite astutely, that the family's 'instinct for song' was shared 'in very unequal proportions; requiring in the case of Acton Bell [Anne], the indulgences of affection ... and rising in that of Ellis [Emily], into an inspiration' (*Athenaeum*, 4 July 1846). The *Spectator* was more critical, accusing the authors of ignoring 'the nature of poetical composition'.

LATER CRITICISM

Much of what has been written about the Brontës is of a largely biographical nature. Many authors have been concerned to relate their lives and unusual family background to their literature. The poems have often been seen as clues to understanding their lives rather than as literary texts in their own right. Even so, far less has been written about the Brontës' poetry than about their novels, and what little has been written has mostly been about Emily, who is almost always rated more highly than her siblings. Emily Dickinson (1830–86) admired Emily's poems, calling her 'gigantic Emily Brontë'. Algernon Charles Swinburne (1837–1909) found in the

> **CONTEXT**
>
> Robert Southey was in his youth a political radical, as well as a friend of Coleridge, but modified his view to the point where he was granted an annual allowance by the Tory government in 1807. He was appointed Poet Laureate in 1813, and was accused by Byron and Hazlitt of betraying his political principles.

 CHECK THE POEM

Emily Dickinson shared with Emily Brontë an independence of mind, a tendency towards reclusiveness, and a concern with death and the immortal. See, for example, 'It was not death, for I stood up' (1891).

SPIRITUAL YEARNING continued

'passionate great genius of Emily Bronte ... a dark, unconscious instinct as of primitive nature-worship'. Virginia Woolf (1882–1941) thought that Emily's poems might outlast *Wuthering Heights* in fame. In contrast to those critics who have accused her of being self-indulgent and melodramatic, Woolf wrote of her, 'The impulse which urged her to create was not her own suffering or her own injuries.' Contrasting her with Charlotte, Woolf writes that Emily possessed 'the gigantic ambition' to comment on the relationship between 'the whole human race' and 'the eternal powers' (*Collected Essays*, i. p. 189).

May Sinclair (1863–1946), in her essay *The Three Brontës* (1912), writes of Anne: 'Her simple poems, at their bitterest, express no more than a frail agony, an innocent dismay.' She rates Charlotte's poetry only a little more highly:

> Of Charlotte Brontë's poems there is not much to say. They are better poems than Branwell's or Anne's, but that does not make them very good. Still, they are interesting, and they are important, because they are the bridge by which Charlotte Brontë passed into her own dominion. She took Wordsworth with his poems and ballads for her guide, and he misled her and delayed her on her way, and kept her a long time standing on her bridge. For in her novels, and her novels only, Charlotte was a poet. In her poems she is a novelist, striving and struggling for expression in a cramped form, an imperfect and improper medium.

Like other critics, Sinclair has most praise for Emily, focusing on her mystical vision of the universe and her ability to express it. She compares Emily with that earlier **Romantic** visionary, William Blake:

> It is doubtful if she ever read a line of Blake; yet it is Blake that her poems perpetually recall, and it is Blake's vision that she has reached there. She too knew what it was

> To see a world in a grain of sand,
>   And a Heaven in a wild flower,
> To hold Infinity in the palm of your hand,
>   And Eternity in an hour.

CHECK THE POEM

May Sinclair quotes a **stanza** from William Blake's *Auguries of Innocence* (1803). The poem also comments on cruelty to animals, dishonesty, and human suffering.

She sees by a flash what he saw continuously; but it is by the same light she sees it and wins her place among the mystics.

Sinclair also makes an important point – taken up by later critics, including Derek Stanford and Janet Gezari (see **Further reading: Criticism**) – that Emily was pulled in two directions. Her mind '…swung between its vision of transparent unity and its love of earth for earth's sake'. Sinclair particularly raises the ambivalence of 'The Night-Wind' and the striving for the transcendental in 'The Prisoner'. Her praise of 'No coward soul is mine' is more muted:

I do not think it is by any means the finest poem that Emily Bronte ever wrote. It has least of her matchless, incommunicable quality. There is one verse, the fifth, that recalls almost painfully the frigid poets of Deism of the eighteenth century. But even that association cannot destroy or contaminate its superb sincerity and dignity.

QUESTION

Do you agree with Sinclair about the weakness of **stanza** 5 in 'No coward soul is mine'?

F. R. Leavis also singled out Emily for praise in his 1936 work, *Revaluation: Tradition and Development in English Poetry*:

Emily Brontë has hardly yet had full justice as a poet; I will record, without offering it as a checked and deliberated critical judgement, the remembered impression that her 'Cold in the Earth' ['Remembrance'] is the finest poem in the nineteenth-century part of the *Oxford Book of English Verse*.

In a later article, however ('Reality and Sincerity', *Scrutiny*, 19, 2 [1952]), Leavis changes his mind and calls the poem insincere, on the grounds that it does not reflect actual life experience – adding that she could not be expected to write convincingly about something outside of her own experience. For Leavis, the poem's declamatory tone is an indicator of false emotion couched in rhetoric. He writes:

Emily Brontë conceives a situation in order to have the satisfaction of a disciplined imaginative exercise: the satisfaction of dramatising herself in a tragic role – an attitude nobly impressive, of sternly controlled passionate desolation.

QUESTION

Do you think a poet has to have had an experience in order to write about it with sincerity? Does it matter to 'Remembrance' that Emily Brontë had never had a lover, let alone outlived one by fifteen years?

CHECK THE NET

For an excellent site on the Brontës, with pages on Haworth and a page of useful links (under Resources), see the Brontë Parsonage Museum's **www. bronte.org.uk**

The marks of the imaginative self-projection that is insufficiently informed by experience are there in the poem.

Later, in 1988, the critic Maureen Peek O Toole commented: 'Leavis's remarks are as patronising as they are irrelevant.' She argues persuasively that Leavis has fallen into a pitfall which 'bedevils studies of Emily Brontë's poetry' – that of 'confusing the speaker with the actual historic poet' (*Aspects of Lyric in the Poetry of Emily Brontë*, Rodopi, 1988).

CONTEMPORARY APPROACHES

Stevie Davies echoes the general view when she comments on the initially dismal sales of the sisters' poems: 'yet none of the Brontës is a negligible poet, and Emily is a great one' (Introduction to *The Brontë Sisters: Selected Poems*, Carcanet, 1976). Although the four siblings have their individual qualities, their similarities are often the basis of negative criticism. Stevie Davies is not alone in noting their repetitive vocabulary and ideas – their tendency towards dreariness, despair, dungeons and desolation, and their reliance on formal metre and rhyme. Tom Winnifrith and Edward Chitham note their similarity of topics and the fact that 'their verse forms, so often taken from their late eighteenth-century masters, are often the same'. They note the 'straightforward vocabulary' and 'conventional poetic word order', concluding:

> The sisters did not make any attempt at radical innovation, apparently taking the view that poetic form was a ready-made bottle into which their home-brewed ale might be poured. (*Charlotte and Emily Brontë*, Literary Lives, Macmillan, 1989)

Most critics, however, agree that Emily most often rises above these limitations (though perhaps least in her vocabulary). Pamela Norris, in her introduction to the Everyman edition, quotes John Drinkwater's claims that both Emily and Branwell 'had the wildness, the sense of loneliness, the ache for some indefinable thing called freedom, that mark the poet from infancy', but adds that, in her opinion, 'Emily is consistently a better poet than Branwell, whose writing is too often vitiated by the failure of conviction that was characteristic of his behaviour in everyday life'.

Few would accuse Emily of a 'failure of conviction', but the idea that she did at times suffer from this is part of one of the most interesting critiques, by Derek Stanford (*Emily Bronte: Her Life and Works*, Arrow Books, 1985), of Emily's poetry. He feels that when she is truly in tune with her subject matter, her poetic form becomes one with it. At other times, however, in her lesser poems, because she has such a fine musical ear for verse, it is often possible to fault her ideas and diction while admiring the rhythmical form. Stanford identifies her main concerns as being fourfold: stoicism (in the popular sense of endurance); pantheism (a doctrine which identifies the divine with natural phenomena; see **Reading the Brontës' poetry**); Christianity; and 'a form of personal quietism', by which he means her particular approach to mysticism. Stanford sees a couplet in 'To Imagination' as especially pertinent to an understanding of Emily's poetic process:

> So hopeless is the world without,
> The world within I doubly prize. (7–8)

This **couplet**, says Stanford, neatly sums up Emily's response to the gulf between the ideal and reality. His theory is that Emily's poetic process can be seen as a three-runged ladder. The first step, her initial reaction to harsh reality, is stoicism. However, a joyless endurance of one's lot is hard to bear, and so her next step is to rejoice in nature: this is her pantheism. The third rung consists of her striving for the transcendental. Her problem, as May Sinclair identified, was that she was still pulled towards the earth, through nature. Her pantheism, in Stanford's opinion, is the only quality she shares with most of the best nineteenth-century poets. He identifies this two-way pull as manifesting in a day/night dialectic in her poems – the best example being 'Stars'. He also identifies this ambivalence between earthly life and eternity as the major theme of 'Death'. On the merits of 'No coward soul is mine', he disagrees with May Sinclair's view, holding that the strong music of the poem carries its abstract nouns (for example, Faith, Fear and infinity),

QUESTION

How far do you feel that Emily's poems are always better than Branwell's?

CONTEXT

Carl Gustav Jung (1875–1961) was a psychoanalyst who at one time shared much of Freud's thinking. However, he diverged from Freud. He coined the psychoanalytic terms *animus* (the male aspect in a woman's psyche) and *anima* (the female or mother aspect of a man's psyche).

CONTEXT

The Duke of Wellington was the leader of the British armed forces fighting against Napoleon. He finally defeated Napoleon at Waterloo in 1815. Wellington became a reactionary conservative figure, and a key member of the Tory Party, becoming Prime Minister in 1828.

which would otherwise make the poem seem too cerebral. He admires its 'deep emotion and intellectual clarity'.

Among modern critics, a more interesting offshoot of the biographical approach to the Brontës' poetry is the psychoanalytical one. Bettina L. Knapp, for example, in *The Brontës: Branwell, Anne, Emily, Charlotte* (Continuum, 1992), presents a critique of the Brontës' poetry based on Jungian psychology. Of Anne's poetry, Knapp notes her loneliness, alienation and sense of inferiority. She also compares her later poems, with their religious anxieties, with her more joyful, hopeful and imaginative Gondal poems (not included in the Everyman selection), such as her love poem 'Alexandria and Zenobia'. She asks, 'Was poetry a compensatory device for Anne?', suggesting that, for Anne, poetry was therapeutic rather than being the work of an artistically compelled genius. Knapp thinks that Charlotte's decision to name the toy soldier Branwell gave her 'The Duke of Wellington' sheds light on her basic conservatism and respect for authority. Knapp comments on Emily's poetry, showing that she was torn by 'raging antagonistic powers within her being', and that she sought psychic release in imagination, as shown in the poem 'To Imagination'. She sees 'Come hither, child' as being about Emily's own lonely and distressing early years. Elsewhere she echoes other critics who have focused on Emily's transcendentalism, but gives it a psychological slant:

> To seek to live in the world of the imagination while divesting oneself of the mundane is, in a certain sense, to yearn for death (*thanatos*) in order to return to the fullness (*pleroma*) of God. For Emily, the existential sphere with all of its commitments, obligations, and commonplaces meant imprisonment in consciousness and in linear time, form, and matter. (p. 104)

Bettina Knapp is perhaps most interesting on the subject of Branwell, since so little has been written about him. She writes that he cultivated imagination and emotion, not reason, was self-indulgent and egotistical, and spent his life looking back mournfully on his childhood. She puts this down in part to his being spoiled by both his father and his sisters, and by the loss of his mother, and then as having been left by his beloved sister Maria. This left him 'unable to develop a conscious attitude towards woman. In that his projection into women remained inchoate [undeveloped], he was unequal to the task of differentiating or evaluating the various facets of their personalities' (p. 58). His resultant self-pity is a major factor in many of his poems.

Janet Gezari, in *Last Things: Emily Brontë's Poems* (OUP, 2007), argues that it is Emily's very uniqueness that has made feminist critics less interested in her than in poets like Elizabeth Barrett Browning. Unlike those critics who have dwelled on the depressive tendencies in Emily's verse, Gezari asserts that 'Supreme enjoyment – an unqualified affirmation of the joy of being alive – is the core of [Emily] Brontë's poems and is entirely compatible with her intimate knowledge of despair and her unflinching recognition of our human capacity for cruelty and ingratitude'. She suggests that the excess of feeling in Emily's poems may disincline us to think of them as sublime, yet her poems are more genuinely mystical than those of the **Romantics** (such as Wordsworth), and yet also more at ease with the natural world. An interesting insight which Gezari develops is that Emily is concerned 'with endings, and with how we defy, resist, blur, or transcend them'. On a stylistic note, she comments on the recurrence of the word 'again' at the ends of lines, and even at the ends of poems, in Emily's verse (as at the end of 'Remembrance'). This prevents us from feeling that the experience recorded in the poem is over and done with. At times, she points out, feminine line endings (where the stress falls on the penultimate syllable) help to create a sense of something unfinished. Similarly, Emily Brontë's poems often have circular structures and 'outcomes that resemble openings rather than endings: If time is a prison that confines us, then Brontë's poems return again and again both to the prison site and to the prison break'.

As Janet Gezari points out, very little has been written about Emily's poems from a feminist viewpoint – and even less has been written about the other siblings' poetry from this viewpoint. Feminist critiques, and to some extent Marxist ones, might focus on a number of threads in the poems. The poems of Charlotte and Emily often focus on power relations. For example, in Charlotte's 'Mementos', the woman in the story is a wife who has been

QUESTION

Do you think it likely that Branwell would have become a better poet had he not lost first his mother and then his older sister Maria? Did he lack the talent of his sisters, or just the application?

CHECK THE BOOK

Some have argued that the idea of feminism was initiated and shaped by Mary Wollstonecraft's *A Vindication of the Rights of Woman*, 1792 (Penguin edition, 2004).

QUESTION

Which other of the Brontës' poems could you interpret from a feminist perspective?

exploited and abandoned by her husband. 'He saw my heart's woe' presents male domination in two forms – the rejecting man 'stirless as a tower' (9), who controls by refusing to respond, and the same thing embodied in a religion with a male deity. Charlotte tries to split off 'bad' male domination in the form of 'The Granite God' (15) from 'good' male domination in the form of the 'King eternal', but the result is unconvincing. In Emily's 'The Prisoner', it is a male captor who controls a female prisoner. One interpretation of the poem could be that the prisoner seeks the only escape from this domination available to her, in death. One could also view Anne's religious impulse as the result of a need to appease patriarchy (male authority), in the form of her own father and the Christian God.

PART FIVE

BACKGROUND

THE BRONTËS' LIVES AND WORKS

A powerful and deep-rooted Brontë myth has developed, stemming
initially from Elizabeth Gaskell's biography of Charlotte, according
to which the Brontës grew up in wild seclusion in a remote
moorland hamlet, untutored by the influence of polite society. This
image, largely the result of Mrs Gaskell wanting to provide an
excuse for what some critics saw as the unladylike 'coarseness' of
the Brontës' novels, has to some extent distorted views of the
Brontës, although it is actually far from being the whole truth.
Although the Brontës did live on the edge of the moors, Haworth
was a lively industrial town whose population more than doubled
between 1801 and 1851 to 3,365. It had its own orchestra, and its
Foresters Hall hosted public lectures on such diverse subjects as
social change and phrenology (the attempt to determine character
and intellect from skull shape). Keighley, four miles away, had a
Mechanics' Institute where lectures also took place, and a library
from which the family borrowed books. On one occasion, in 1840,
the three sisters and Charlotte's friend Ellen Nussey walked there
and back to hear their father's curate, William Weightman, lecture
on the classics. The family was fairly self-sufficient socially, but not
entirely isolated. Even as children, the Brontës were able to read
newspapers and magazines, which influenced their own early
literary efforts, as well as a wide range of books. In addition, all
three girls had spells at boarding school. Many writers have
followed the lead given by Mrs Gaskell in interpreting the Brontës'
work in terms of the sisters' own experiences. However, these
experiences should be considered alongside broader social and
literary influences.

CHECK THE BOOK

Emily's love of the moors can be seen in *Wuthering Heights*, which Charlotte called 'moorish, and wild, and knotty as the root of heath'.

THE BRONTË FAMILY

Patrick Brontë came from a poor Northern Irish family, but his
considerable talent enabled him to overcome his social
disadvantages to win a place at Cambridge University. On
graduating, he obtained a position as curate in Hartshead,

CHECK THE BOOK

Anne's religious feelings and desire to do some moral good in the world inspired *The Tenant of Wildfell Hall*.

Yorkshire. He was an Anglican, but his wife Maria, whom he married in 1812, came from a Methodist family in Cornwall. The couple produced six children in eight years: Maria (1813), Elizabeth (1815), Charlotte (1816), Branwell (1817), Emily (1818) and Anne (1820). The family moved to Haworth in 1819, where Emily, especially, enjoyed roaming the local moors.

Although the moorland offered fresh air and exercise, disease was common in Haworth, especially the tuberculosis that took the lives of five of the Brontë children – all except Charlotte. (According to the 1850 Babbage Report, 41.6 per cent of children in Haworth died before the age of six.) Also contrary to the impression created by Mrs Gaskell's account, the Brontë children were aware of contemporary issues. The story of the Luddite riots which had occurred in nearby Liversedge in 1812 was recounted to the children by Patrick Brontë – to resurface in Charlotte's novel *Shirley*. Workers were exploited, and poverty was commonplace. The children heard about such social problems from their father and witnessed some of them at first hand. The influence of family on the Brontë children was, however, probably stronger than that of the locality. The eldest, Maria, was only seven when their mother died. Their mother's sister, Aunt Branwell, came to keep house and look after the children. Anne, as the youngest, shared her aunt's bed and bonded with her more closely than the others did, absorbing more of her strict Methodist doctrine and morality.

Patrick Brontë was an intelligent man with vigorous opinions. Mrs Gaskell's claims that he was an overbearing figure who burned the children's boots, angrily sawed the legs off furniture, and regularly fired a pistol to discharge his anger, have some basis in truth but are much exaggerated. By other accounts he was a caring and supportive father who discussed current affairs with his children, read them newspaper articles and encouraged their own reading. In addition Maria read reports of parliamentary debates to her younger siblings. The children grew up arguing about the relative merits of great leaders such as the Duke of Wellington – Charlotte's hero. In short, they enjoyed an atmosphere of lively intellectual stimulation, only somewhat removed from the rest of society.

EDUCATION AND EARLY WORKS

In 1824 Patrick Brontë sent his four eldest girls to the Reverend Wilson's 'School for Clergymen's Daughters' at Cowan Bridge, on the edge of the Yorkshire Dales. The education itself was paid for by charity, but parents paid £14 a year for a girl's board and lodging. The school taught 'history, geography, the use of the globes, grammar, writing and arithmetic, all kinds of needlework, and the nicer kinds of household work'. Yet it was poorly run and spartan to the point of real deprivation. The buildings were cold and damp, and the diet inadequate. The school placed an emphasis on developing humility in the girls by impressing on them their lowly position and their debt to society. Mrs Gaskell describes the cruelty with which a teacher called Miss Scatcherd treated the sick Maria. Even a more sympathetic teacher, Miss Temple, advised the girls to endure their lot quietly.

Weakened by the school regime, Maria and Elizabeth died from tuberculosis in 1825. Shocked at their deaths, and by reports of food contamination, Patrick Brontë removed Charlotte and Emily from the school after a term. Joined in loss, the remaining children created intense imaginary worlds. They made up and acted out plays, which developed into stories and poems about these worlds, recorded in tiny books in handwriting so small as to be almost impossible to read. These literary worlds gradually matured, eventually giving rise to some of Emily's finest poems.

In 1831 the fifteen-year-old Charlotte was sent to a more enlightened school, Roe Head, near Huddersfield, run by Margaret Wooler. Here Charlotte made two lifelong friends, Ellen Nussey and Mary Taylor. Unfortunately Patrick could only afford for her to stay for eighteen months, after which she came home to pass on what she had learned to her sisters. Patrick himself took charge of Branwell's education. Charlotte described this at the time as a 'delightful, though somewhat monotonous' phase of her life. In 1835 she returned to Roe Head as a teacher, and her poems 'Retrospection' date from this time, expressing her homesickness and loneliness. Emily accompanied her to the school as a pupil but returned home after only two months, desperately homesick for the moors, to be replaced by Anne.

CONTEXT

The loss of their mother strongly affected all three sisters, notwithstanding Anne's relationship with her aunt. Almost every Brontë novel has a motherless main character, and this is a particular feature of Charlotte's work.

 CHECK THE BOOK

The gentle Maria was to become the model for the consumptive Helen Burns in *Jane Eyre*, the Reverend Wilson for Brocklehurst, and Miss Temple for a character of the same name.

 CHECK THE BOOK

There is probably something of Patrick Brontë in Charlotte's portrayal of Monsieur Paul in *Villette* and Anne's Reverend Millward in *The Tenant of Wildfell Hall*.

One might regard Branwell as an underachiever in such a gifted family. However, he played an important role in the flowering of his sisters' work, as well as producing significant poems of his own. It seems likely that he suffered under the strain of his father's expectations, and perhaps even his sisters' hopes for him. He seems to have been torn between a high opinion of his own talents and a debilitating sense of inferiority. The latter was exacerbated by his appearance, which he often caricatured in drawings. His small stature made him wear his red hair piled up to give an impression of height. It also led him to join the Haworth boxing club, which met at the Black Bull Inn – which became a favourite haunt of his. His views of his own talents led him, in 1836, to try to persuade *Blackwood's Magazine* to sack one of its major contributors and hire him in his place. He also wrote to Wordsworth, dismissing other poets and recommending himself (see **Critical perspectives: Early reception**).

Branwell managed to set himself up as a portrait painter in Bradford, and to secure some commissions. The image by which we best know the sisters is a painting by Branwell, the so-called 'Pillar Portrait', dating from around 1835. Branwell evidently changed his mind about including himself in this portrait, and replaced himself with a pillar. However, he had never really learned to mix paint properly, and so his attempts have faded, revealing once more a faint image of the artist. This same inexperience was a factor limiting his professional success. By 1839 he was drinking heavily, and in 1840 he lost a job as tutor. He was dismissed from the post of railway clerk for accounting 'irregularities' – perhaps embezzlement. Through Anne, he obtained a post as tutor at Thorp Green, the home of the wealthy Robinson family, where Anne was a governess. After a further two and a half years, however, he was dismissed, apparently for having an affair with the lady of the house, Mrs Robinson, seventeen years his senior. In a letter addressed in a shaky hand to his friend Francis Grundy (of 'The man who will not know another'), Branwell gives his version of how the affair started. He was, he claims, moved by his admiration for Lydia Robinson, her warmth towards him, and his distress at 'the heartless and unmanly manner in which she was treated by an eunuch-like fellow [her husband] who though possessed of such a treasure never even

CHECK THE NET
Branwell's portrait of his sisters, with himself as a ghostly image, is in the National Portrait Gallery in London and can be seen at **www.npg.org.uk**, along with another portrait by Branwell of Emily.

occupied the same apartment with her'. In 1846 Mr Robinson died, but Branwell's hopes that Lydia would marry him were dashed. The poetic outcome was 'Penmaenmawr', and the personal one was Branwell's alcoholic and opiated decline. One can also speculate that during this time, perhaps seeking solace, he fathered a child – which died in infancy, and to whom he addressed 'Epistle From a Father to a Child in Her Grave'. Depressed, his constitution and immune system weakened, he contracted tuberculosis, of which he died in 1848.

CHARLOTTE AND EMILY IN BRUSSELS

In 1842, financed by Aunt Branwell, Charlotte and Emily left for Brussels to study at the Pensionnat Heger. Its principal, Constantin Heger, was a forceful, emotionally intense and short-tempered man. He regarded Emily as more intelligent than Charlotte, but he preferred Charlotte's more amenable nature. The girls were hired for another six months as *au pair*, but this was interrupted by the death of their Aunt Branwell. After the funeral, Charlotte returned to the Pensionnat to teach. Frail and still shy, she was hardly suited to teaching. Added to this, she fell in love with Heger – who rejected her. Charlotte returned home in misery, later writing about her bitter experience in 'He saw my heart's woe'.

HISTORICAL AND SOCIAL BACKGROUND

The Brontës lived in eventful and rapidly changing times. Their father had been born in 1777, twelve years before the outbreak of the French Revolution, an event which shook Europe and led to the Napoleonic Wars. These ended at Waterloo in 1815 with the defeat of Napoleon by the Duke of Wellington. Charlotte was born less than a year later. Years of economic hardship followed, together with social unrest countered by government repression – to which Romantic poets such as Shelley responded with verse and essays urging political reform. The Parliamentary Reform Act of 1832, and the abolition of slavery in the British Empire in 1833, indicated that change was under way. Some social improvements were also made as a result of campaigning, such as the Factory Acts of 1833 and

---

CONTEXT

While Emily and Anne died in 1848 and 1849, Charlotte remained living with her father, accepting the hand in marriage of his curate Arthur Bell Nicholls in 1854. Charlotte died in early pregnancy the following year, and Arthur stayed living at the Parsonage with Patrick until the latter's death in 1861.

CHECK THE BOOK

Heger was the model for Monsieur Paul in *Villette* (Charlotte's name for Brussels), Mme Heger for Madame Beck. The description of Lucy Snowe's visit to a Catholic confessional records Charlotte own desperate visit. *The Professor* is also based closely on Charlotte's Brussels experience.

1844. Soon after the start of Victoria's reign, however, the mass working-class and lower middle-class movement of Chartism began, demanding universal male suffrage (the right to vote for all men), the secret ballot, and pay for MPs. When the Brontë sisters' *Poems* was published in 1846, their father's native land of Ireland was in the grip of the Great Famine (1845–52), caused by potato blight and met largely by government indifference.

Considering how interested the Brontës were as children in national events portrayed in newspapers, it is surprising that their poetry is almost entirely introspective, and seems to bear no relation to these events at all. The Gondal poems perhaps draw on the broad drama of the Napoleonic Wars, but not in any real historical sense. The novels also display some awareness of social differences: the heroine of *Jane Eyre* is keenly aware of her social disadvantages, and in *Wuthering Heights* it is striking that Heathcliff, a Liverpool street urchin, becomes master of the house. However, only Charlotte's novel *Shirley* (1850) makes a deliberate effort to deal with social issues, although it is set during the Napoleonic Wars rather than its own time.

CHECK THE BOOK

In both *Wuthering Heights* and *The Tenant of Wildfell Hall* men refer to, and treat, their wives as their property. In *Jane Eyre*, Charlotte wrote: 'women feel just as men feel; they need exercise for their faculties, and a field for their efforts as much as their brothers do' (Ch. 12).

One can more readily find indications in the Brontës' poems of the position of women in early Victorian society. Despite having had more of an education than many women of their day, the Brontë sisters were well aware of the restraints on women in the male-dominated society in which they lived. Women of their class were expected to be decorative, and accomplished in genteel arts – such as music and sewing – that would please their husbands; they were not educated for careers. Moreover, they had no political power and, if married, no legal rights. A woman could not obtain a divorce until 1857 (the year in which Charlotte died), and until 1870 her property became her husband's on marriage. The Brontë sisters' own career prospects were limited to becoming a governess or a schoolteacher. One could see the role of powerful women such as Augusta in Emily's Gondal poems, for example 'F. De Samara to A. G. A.', as a reaction to this situation. The fact that they considered authorship as an occupation is not so surprising when one considers the alternatives.

Another feature of Victorian life was its strongly Christian ideology. There were many non-conformist Christian groups, but to subscribe to Christianity in some form was the norm. Anne was particularly influenced by Calvinist doctrine, which in its most extreme form taught that only a pre-ordained 'elect' group would enter heaven. Emily was the least conventionally Christian of the siblings – although Branwell declared himself an atheist, before apparently returning to his faith late in his life, as shown in 'Oh Thou, whose beams were most withdrawn' and 'O God! while I in pleasure's wiles'. Despite the widespread belief in Christianity, it clashed with many of the values of the Industrial Revolution and the burgeoning commercial world. Wealthy industrialists and businessmen who considered themselves to be firm Christians exploited the poor, justifying themselves by regarding poverty as God's will, or by insisting that the poor only had themselves to blame, and that their situation was caused by alcohol and general fecklessness. Such contradictions are perhaps hinted at in Emily's 'The Prisoner'.

> **CONTEXT**
>
> The plight of single women became more acute in the mid-nineteenth century as their numbers increased owing to a higher male infant mortality rate, emigration and men marrying later.

LITERARY BACKGROUND

The Brontë children read widely, especially Sir Walter Scott's novels, and much poetry. In 1834 Charlotte recommended to a friend: 'Milton, Shakespeare, Thomson, Goldsmith, Pope (if you will, though I don't admire him), Scott, Byron, Campbell, Wordsworth and Southey.' The epic grandeur of Milton's *Paradise Lost* and the tragedies of Shakespeare are evident in the cosmology and the plot of *Wuthering Heights*. The bitter loss and desire for revenge of Milton's Satan can be detected in the speaker of 'F. De Samara to A. G. A'. Some of Emily's poems recall the rhythms and **imagery** of Shakespeare's tragedies, while some of Anne's suggest his descriptive pastoral passages. The world-weariness found in all three of the older siblings echoes that of some of Shakespeare's tragic figures, such as Hamlet:

> O, that this too too solid flesh would melt
> Thaw and resolve itself into a dew!
> Or that the Everlasting had not fix'd

His canon 'gainst self-slaughter! O God! God!
How weary, stale, flat and unprofitable,
Seem to me all the uses of this world!
Fie on't! ah fie! 'tis an unweeded garden,
That grows to seed; things rank and gross in nature
Possess it merely. (Act 1, scene 2)

Hamlet's desire to rid himself of his body and leave the world behind, together with his choice of vegetable imagery, reminds us of Emily, for example in 'Death'.

EIGHTEENTH-CENTURY POETRY

Some eighteenth-century poets were probably an influence on the Brontës – Charlotte herself names James Thomson (1700–48), famous for his long pastoral poem 'The Seasons' (1830). All four strive at times for the strong sense of atmosphere created by Thomas Gray (1716–71) in his 'Elegy Written in a Country Churchyard', which uses a twilight setting to induce a contemplative mood. Charlotte's 'The Teacher's Monologue' and 'The Autumn day its course has run' contain hints of this poem, as does Branwell's 'On Caroline'. It is also known that Anne was influenced by William Cowper (1731–1800), both in the sentiments of his religious poems and in his style. His verse forms and relatively simple diction, together with his confessional style, may have influenced Emily too. See, for example, 'The Shrubbery: Written in a Time of Affliction' (1782):

Oh, happy shades – to me unblest,
    Friendly to peace, but not to me,
How ill the scene that offers rest,
    And heart that cannot rest, agree!
That glassy stream, that spreading pine,
    Those alders quivering to the breeze,
Might sooth a soul less hurt than mine,
    And please, if any thing could please.

ROMANTIC POETRY

All four siblings were influenced by the **Romantic** poets, most obviously William Wordsworth. Although it was Branwell who

**CHECK
THE POEM**
One of Thomas Gray's more entertaining poems is his 'Ode on the Death of a Favourite Cat Drowned in a Tub of Gold Fishes'.

wrote his rather sycophantic letter to the great man in the hope that his own poetry would thereby get a leg-up in the literary world (see **Critical perspectives: Early reception**), it is Emily and Anne whose poems have more in common with his. Wordsworth's deliberately unaffected diction and feeling for profound truths revealed in nature can be compared with Emily's pantheistic poems (see **Reading the Brontës' poetry**), such as 'Loud without the wind was roaring' and 'The blue bell is the sweetest flower', and certain lines of hers seem to echo Wordsworth both in style and concept – for example in 'Alone I sat': 'The solemn joy around me stealing/ In that divine untroubled hour' (9–10). One could also compare Anne's 'The Bluebell' with Wordsworth's 'Daffodils'.

CHECK THE POEM
Wordsworth uses the phrase 'solemn joy' in his 'The Morning of the Day Appointed for a General Thanksgiving, January 18, 1816'.

Another influence on the Brontës, with whom they may be compared, is Percy Bysshe Shelley (1792–1822), the supreme poet of Romantic individualism. Like Emily and Anne he sometimes writes of spiritual joy inspired by nature, as in his 'Ode to a Skylark'. The following **stanza** has something of Emily in its sensory appeal and its evocation of joy:

> The pale purple even
>   Melts around thy flight;
> Like a star of heaven,
>   In the broad daylight
> Thou art unseen, but yet I hear they shrill delight –

It is not Emily's style, however, to write a poem focusing so closely on a single bird. For all her love of nature, she never writes about it without also writing about the emotions it inspires in her. One could also compare some of her poems, such as 'Loud without the wind was roaring', or Anne's 'Lines Composed in a Wood on a Windy Day', with Shelley's 'Ode to the West Wind'. However, once again, Shelley's focus is on the wind, while the sisters are more concerned with the effect of nature on themselves. Shelley, too, had a Romantic concern with national politics which was not shared by any of the Brontës. In fact, in some ways, Emily has more in common with John Keats (1795–1821), whose poetry is often more sensual and introspective than Shelley's. His 'Ode to a Nightingale' has similarities with Emily's 'The Night-Wind', although Keats's

CHECK THE POEM
Unlike the Brontës, Shelley sometimes wrote poems entirely focused on his interpretation of an external subject, rather than on his emotional response to it. One example is 'Ozymandias'.

lines of **pentameter** are more drawn out. His 'La Belle Dame Sans
Merci', with its mournful–magical mood and medieval setting, has
similarities with some of the Gondal poems.

Lord Byron (1788–1824) is another influence, both in his personal
legend and his verse. His image chimed with the wild, dark,
individualistic characters of Heathcliff in *Wuthering Heights* and
Rochester in *Jane Eyre*, and corresponding characters in the Gondal
poems. His verse also has qualities in common with Emily's poems,
especially those with a Gondal setting. One could, for example,
compare his **narrative** poem 'The Prisoner of Chillon' with Emily's
'The Prisoner'. For example:

> It was at length the same to me,
> Fettered or fetterless to be,
>   I learned to love despair.
> And thus when they appeared at last,
> And all my bonds aside were cast,
> These heavy walls to me had grown
> A hermitage – and all my own!

**CHECK
THE POEM**

Felicia Hemans's
most famous poem
now is 'Casabianca',
more commonly
known as 'The boy
stood on the
burning deck',
based on a heroic
incident in the
Battle of the Nile
(1798), in which a
French ship was
attacked by the
English under Lord
Nelson.

Another poet almost certainly read by the Brontë sisters, extremely
popular at the time but now largely forgotten, is Felicia Hemans
(1793–1835), who was admired by Wordsworth and attracted the
attention of Shelley. Her poems often border on the sentimental and
patriotic. If she influenced any of the Brontës, it was perhaps
Charlotte in her earlier verse.

VICTORIAN POETRY

Looking back to the eighteenth century in their verse forms, and to
the **Romantics** in their themes, the Brontës in many ways stand out
from the rest of early **Victorian** poetry. In particular, their poems
are far more personal than those of other Victorians, although
Charlotte and Anne at times display a typically Victorian concern
with Christian faith as the ultimate consolation in a suffering world.
Among Victorians, Emily is probably unique in her combination of
pantheism and mysticism. The emotion in her poems could be
compared with Elizabeth Barrett Browning (1806–61), and there are
some similarities with early poems by Alfred, Lord Tennyson, such

as 'Mariana', especially in its refrain, which rhymes 'dreary' with 'aweary'. However, Tennyson is not afraid to use mundane details such as creaking door hinges, and 'the mouldering wainscot'. These are generally absent from Brontë poems, except for the curtains, pillow and fly in Emily's 'Stars'. One could compare this with Tennyson's lines:

> All day within the dreamy house,
>   The doors upon their hinges creaked;
> The blue fly sung in the pane; the mouse
>   Behind the mouldering wainscot shrieked,
> Or from the crevice peered about.

This is a far more domestic scene than any of the Brontës would paint.

One way in which the Brontës are more Victorian than Romantic, however, is in their preoccupation with death, especially when it is presented as part of the **gothic** genre. One could compare Charlotte's 'Mementos' with Robert Browning's 'My Last Duchess', which has a similarly gothic mood and narrative form. Elizabeth Barrett Browning had something of this same interest in death, as did the American admirer of Emily Brontë's poems, Emily Dickinson (see **Critical perspectives: Later criticism**).

PROSE INFLUENCES

Unfortunately, none of the Brontës kept diaries, so we have no reliable record of their reading. However, we do know that only Charlotte survived long enough to be personally involved in the Victorian literary scene. We know that she disliked Charles Dickens, but admired William Thackeray (1811–63), author of *Catherine* (1839) and *Vanity Fair* (1848). When Thackeray read *Jane Eyre*, he commented, 'Who the author can be, I can't guess; if a woman she knows her language better than most ladies do, or has had a classical education' (quoted by Juliet Barker in *The Brontës*, Phoenix Press, 1994). Charlotte met Thackeray and corresponded with him. She even dedicated the second edition of *Jane Eyre* to him. Unfortunately, to her acute embarrassment, this led to the rumour that Rochester's supposedly mad wife was modelled on

QUESTION

Do you feel that the Brontës' poems would be improved by the inclusion of more everyday details, such as Tennyson includes in 'Mariana'?

CHECK THE POEM

Elizabeth Barrett Browning's *Sonnets from the Portuguese* is a collection of forty-four love sonnets. Their intimacy and emotion in some ways echo the poems of the Brontës.

CHECK THE BOOK

A dramatic work that may have caught the Brontës' attention around the time that they were writing their novels and poetry was the anonymous play, *Maria Marten, or Murder in the Red Barn* (1840), a melodrama based on a real-life crime of passion that occurred in 1827. The murder of Maria by her jealous lover William Corder has similarities with the intense passion of Emily's novel and some of her poems.

Thackeray's housekeeper. Charlotte also became friends with Elizabeth (Mrs) Gaskell, who eventually became her biographer. Charlotte's novel *Shirley* (1850) was probably influenced by Gaskell's *Mary Barton* (1848), which deals with the plight of the working class in Manchester, and Gaskell in turn was almost certainly influenced by Charlotte's novels. A later Victorian author who may also have been influenced by Charlotte is Thomas Hardy, whose *Tess of the D'Urbevilles* has some similarities in plot and characterisation with *Jane Eyre*.

Emily may well have been influenced by Mary Shelley's *Frankenstein* (1818), which may have provided the model for her layered narrative within narrative in *Wuthering Heights*, as well as in such poems as 'The Prisoner'. This in turn may have influenced Wilkie Collins's use of multiple first-person narrative in *The Woman in White* (1860) and *The Moonstone* (1868).

Peaks College

World events

1814 Napoleon banished to Elba

1815 Napoleon escapes but is beaten finally at Waterloo

1819 Birth of future Queen Victoria; 'Peterloo' Massacre, Manchester

1820 George III dies; succeeded by Prince Regent, George IV

1821 Cato Street Conspiracy against Cabinet

1822 Turks invade Greece; suicide of Foreign Secretary, Castlereagh

The Brontës' lives

1814 Maria born

1815 Elizabeth born; Patrick curate at Thornton

1816 Charlotte born

1817 (Patrick) Branwell born

1818 Emily born

1820 Anne born; Patrick made perpetual curate of Haworth; family moves there

1821 Mrs Maria Brontë dies of cancer

1824 Maria and Elizabeth enrol at Cowan Bridge School; Charlotte and Emily join them later

1825 Maria and Elizabeth die of tuberculosis; Charlotte and Emily removed from school

Literary events

1814 Jane Austen, *Mansfield Park*; Walter Scott, *Waverley*; William Wordsworth, 'The Excursion'

1815 Lord Byron, 'Hebrew Melodies'

1816 Austen, *Emma*; P. B. Shelley, 'Alastor'

1818 Austen, *Northanger Abbey* and *Persuasion*; Byron, *Don Juan*; John Keats, 'Endymion'; Scott, *Heart of Midlothian* and *Rob Roy*; Mary Shelley, *Frankenstein*

1820 Keats, 'Ode to a Nightingale'; Scott, *Ivanhoe*; Shelley, 'Prometheus Unbound'

1821 Keats dies; commemorated in Shelley's 'Adonais'

1822 Shelley dies

1824 Byron dies at Missolonghi, in Turko-Greek War; Scott, *Redgauntlet*

World events

1828 Wellington becomes Prime Minister

1830 Revolution in Paris; in Britain William IV succeeds George IV

1832 Reform Act doubles number of voters

1837 William IV succeeded by Victoria

1838 First Chartist petition presented

1839 Coronation of Queen Victoria

The Brontës' lives

1831 Charlotte goes to Roe Head School

1832 Charlotte returns home

1835 Branwell trains for Royal Academy but fails to enter it; Charlotte appointed teacher at Roe Head School; Emily enrols as student there; homesick, she returns home; Anne replaces her

1837 Emily becomes teacher at Law Hill School; Anne becomes ill; she and Charlotte return home; Charlotte resigns her post

1838 Branwell sets up as a portrait painter in Bradford; Emily returns from Law Hill

1839 Anne becomes governess to Ingham family; dismissed after 8 months; Branwell gives up career as artist

Literary events

1828 Scott, *Tales of a Grandfather* and *The Fair Maid of Perth*

1829 Alfred, Lord Tennyson, 'Timbuctoo'

1830 Emily Dickinson and Christina Rossetti born; Tennyson, *Poems, Chiefly Lyrical*

1831 Edgar Allen Poe, *Poems*

1832 Scott dies; Tennyson, 'The Lady of Shalott'

1834 S. T. Coleridge and Charles Lamb (essayist) die

1835 Wordsworth, *Poems*; Robert Browning, 'Paracelsus'

1836 Charles Dickens, *Pickwick Papers*

1838 E. B. Browning, *The Seraphim and Other Poems*

1839 H. W. Longfellow, 'Hyperion' and 'Voices of the Night'; Poe, *The Fall of the House of Usher*

World events	The Brontës' lives	Literary events
1840 Victoria marries Prince Albert	**1840** Anne becomes governess to Robinson family at Thorp Green; Branwell employed as tutor in Broughton-in-Furness, then as clerk in Sowerby Bridge Railway Station	**1840** Robert Browning, 'Sordello'
1841 Lord Melbourne (Whig) succeeded as Prime Minister by Peel (Tory)	**1841** Charlotte governess at Upperwood House, near Leeds; resigns after 8 months	**1841** Dickens, *The Old Curiosity Shop*
1842 Riots and strikes in north of England	**1842** Charlotte and Emily enrol as pupils in the Pensionnat Heger, Brussels; Aunt Branwell dies and Charlotte and Emily return home	**1842** Poe, 'The Masque of the Red Death'
	1843 Charlotte returns to Pensionnat Heger as a teacher; Branwell becomes tutor at Thorp Green	**1843** Robert Southey dies; Tennyson, 'Mort d'Arthur', 'Locksley Hall'; Wordsworth Poet Laureate
	1844 Charlotte comes home, in love with Heger	
1845 Start of Irish Famine	**1845** Anne resigns as governess to Robinson family; Branwell dismissed from Robinson family for affair with Mrs Robinson	
	1846 Publication of *Poems*, by 'Currer, Ellis, and Acton Bell'	
	1847 Charlotte publishes *Jane Eyre*; Anne's *Agnes Grey* and Emily's *Wuthering Heights* published	**1847** W. M. Thackeray, *Vanity Fair*
1848 European revolts, including Paris	**1848** Anne publishes *The Tenant of Wildfell Hall:*	**1848** Mrs Gaskell, *Mary Barton*

World events	The Brontës' lives	Literary events
	1848 (September) Branwell dies of tuberculosis; (December) Emily dies of tuberculosis	
1849 Disraeli leader of Conservative Party	**1849** Anne dies of tuberculosis, Scarborough; Charlotte publishes *Shirley*	**1849** Dickens, *David Copperfield*
		1850 E. B. Browning, *Sonnets from the Portuguese*; Wordsworth dies; Tennyson Poet Laureate
		1851 Herman Melville, *Moby Dick*
1852 Duke of Wellington dies		**1852** Dickens, *Bleak House*
1853 Crimean War begins	**1853** Charlotte publishes *Villette*	**1853** Matthew Arnold, 'The Scholar Gypsy'; Mrs Gaskell, *Ruth* and *Cranford*
	1854 Charlotte marries Arthur Bell Nicholls	**1854** Tennyson, 'The Charge of the Light Brigade'
	1855 Charlotte dies in early pregnancy	**1855** R. Browning, *Men and Women*; Longfellow, *The Song of Hiawatha*; Tennyson, 'Maud'; Walt Whitman, *Leaves of Grass*
1856 Crimean War ends		**1856** Gustave Flaubert, *Madame Bovary*
1857 Indian Mutiny	**1857** Charlotte's *The Professor* is published	**1857** Anthony Trollope, *Barchester Towers*
		1859 Dickens, *A Tale of Two Cities*; George Eliot, *Adam Bede*; Tennyson, 'Idylls of the King'
	1861 Patrick Bronte dies	

NOVELS AND STORIES BY THE BRONTËS

CHARLOTTE BRONTË

Jane Eyre, 1847

Shirley, 1849

Villette, 1853

The Professor, 1857

Tales of Angria, Penguin, 2006

EMILY JANE BRONTË
Wuthering Heights, 1847

ANNE BRONTË
Agnes Grey, 1848

The Tenant of Wildfell Hall, 1848

BIOGRAPHY

Juliet Barker, *The Brontës,* Phoenix Press, 1994
An authoritative, comprehensive biography of the whole family

Elizabeth Gaskell (ed. E. Jay), *The Life of Charlotte Bronte,* Penguin, 1998
A fascinating though not entirely accurate account, which helped to create the myth of the Brontës' isolation

Francis Grundy, *Pictures of the Past,* Griffith & Farran, 1879
An out of print work by Branwell's friend which contains a section describing Branwell

Daphne du Maurier, *The Infernal World of Branwell Brontë,* Virago Press, 2006
A narrative biography by a well-known novelist focusing on Branwell

Joan Rees, *Profligate Son; Branwell Brontë and his Sisters,* Robert Hale, 1986
Draws on extensive documentary evidence to explore Branwell's relationships and the reasons for his decline

CRITICISM

Stevie Davies (ed.), *The Brontë Sisters: Selected Poems*, Carcanet, 1976
   A good selection of the poems, including some well-worth reading but not in the Everyman
   selection, with an insightful introduction looking at each of the sisters in turn

—, 'The Mother Planet', in Angela Leighton (ed.), *Victorian Women Poets*, Blackwell, 1996
   An essay focusing on the importance of earth as a metaphor for the maternal in Emily's poems

Janet Gezari, *The Last Things: Emily Brontë's Poems*, OUP, 2007
   An in-depth study of Emily's poems by a Brontë scholar, aiming to be comprehensive, though
   focusing closely on a number of poems, including 'Remembrance'

Heather Glen (ed.), *The Cambridge Companion to the Brontës*, CUP, 2003
   A complete guide to the Brontës, containing a chapter, 'The Poetry of the Brontës', by Angela Leighton

Philip Henderson (ed.), *The Complete Poems of Emily Brontë*, Folio Society, 1951
   Contains a useful introduction, including a summary of the Gondal saga

Bettina Knapp, *The Brontës: Branwell, Anne, Emily, Charlotte*, Continuum, 1992
   An analysis of the novels and poems based on Jungian psychology

Maureen Peeck-O'Toole, *Aspects of Lyric in the Poetry of Emily Brontë*, Rodopi, 1988
   An authoritative, scholarly and detailed study

Carl Plasa, *Charlotte Brontë*, Palgrave Macmillan (Critical Issues), 2004
   Mostly of interest in relation to the novels, though with some bearing on the poems

Muriel Spark and Derek Stanford, *Emily Brontë: Her Life and Work*, Arrow Books, 1985
   Includes a biographical study by Spark and an excellent analysis of the poems by Stanford

Tom Winnifrith, *The Brontës and their Background: Romance and Reality*, Macmillan, 1988
   Sets the Brontës in context and considers the relation between the myth and the reality

Tom Winnifrith and Edward Chitham, *Charlotte and Emily Brontë*, Macmillan Literary
Lives, 1989
   Explores Emily and Charlotte in context, focusing on the novels but with a chapter on the poems

WIDER READING

For connections and comparisons with the poetry of the Brontës, see the relevant pages of
these Notes (provided in bold below):

ROMANTIC AND VICTORIAN POETRY

William Blake, *Songs of Innocence*, 1789 (p. 31)

Elizabeth Barrett Browning, *Sonnets from the Portuguese*, 1850 (p. 123)

John Clare, *The Rural Muse*, 1835 (pp. 58, 83)

William Cowper, *Poems*, 1782–5 (p. 120) and 1790 (p. 28)

Emily Dickinson, *Collected Poems*, 1890–6 (p. 105)

John Keats, *Poetical Works*, 1834 (pp. 11, 95, 122)

Christina Rossetti, *Goblin Market and Other Poems*, 1862 (p. 90)

Percy Bysshe Shelley, *Posthumous Poems*, 1824 (see also *Percy Bysshe Shelley* [Everyman], 1998) (pp. 34, 35, 84, 91, 121)

Alfred, Lord Tennyson, *Poems, Chiefly Lyrical*, 1830 (pp. 96, 123)

William Wordsworth, *The Prelude*, 1805 (p. 33)

William Wordsworth and Samuel Taylor Coleridge, *Lyrical Ballads*, 1798 (p. 32)

ROMANTIC AND VICTORIAN PROSE AND DRAMA

Anon., *Maria Marten, or Murder in the Red Barn*, 1840 (p. 124)

Wilkie Collins, *The Woman in White*, 1860 (p. 124)

—, *The Moonstone*, 1868 (p. 124)

Thomas Hardy, *Tess of the D'Urbevilles*, 1891 (p. 124)

Mrs Gaskell, *Mary Barton*, 1848 (p. 124)

Ann Radcliffe, *The Italian*, 1797 (p. 8)

Walter Scott, *The Heart of Midlothian*, 1818 (p. 39)

—, *Ivanhoe*, 1819 (p. 39)

Mary Shelley, *Frankenstein*, 1818 (p. 124)

William Makepeace Thackeray, *Vanity Fair*, 1847–8 (p. 123)

MODERN POETRY

Ted Hughes, *Crow*, 1970 (p. 10)

Philip Larkin, *High Windows*, 1974 (p. 15)

alliteration the repetition of the same consonant or a sequence of vowels in a stretch of language, most often at the beginnings of words or on stressed syllables

allegory a story or a situation with two different meanings, where the straightforward meaning on the surface is used to symbolise a deeper meaning underneath. This secondary meaning is often a spiritual or moral one whose values are represented by specific figures, characters or events in the narrative

allusion a passing reference in a work of literature to something outside the text; may include other works of literature, myth, historical facts or biographical detail

anapasestic of metre, having two unstressed syllables followed by one stressed

assonance the use of the same vowel sound with different consonants or the same consonant with different vowel sounds in successive words or stressed syllables in a line of verse

aubade a poetic form, originally a dawn song, typically in which a lover regrets the coming of dawn as necessitating the departure of a lover

caesura rhythmic break or pause in a line of verse

couplet a pair of rhymed lines of any metre

dactyl a metrical foot consisting of a stressed syllable followed by two unstressed syllables

diction an author's word choice

elegy a poem of lamentation, usually focusing on the death of a single person. More generally, the term 'elegy' can also be used to describe any meditative work of poetry

end-stopped of a line of verse the end of which coincides with the end of a sentence or clause

enjambment in poetry, when a sentence runs on from one line to the next, and even from one stanza to the next

framed narrative a narrative containing another narrative within itself, often with both being in the words of first-person narrators

gothic a term originally applied to a medieval architectural style considered to be barbaric and uncivilised. As a later literary genre, the term implies more than a reference to architectural description – gothic literature deals with passion, mystery, supernatural or horror, and usually employs a medieval setting such as a haunted castle or abbey

heroic couplet pair of rhyming lines of iambic pentameter

hexameter line of verse with six metrical feet

homophone word similar in sound but different in spelling and meaning from another

iambic pentameter a line of poetry consisting of five iambic feet (iambic consisting of a weak syllable followed by a strong one)

imagery descriptive language which uses images to make actions, objects and characters more vivid in the reader's mind. **Metaphors** and **similes** are examples of imagery

irony the humorous or sarcastic use of words to imply the opposite of what they normally mean; incongruity between what might be expected and what actually happens; the ill-timed arrival of an event that had been hoped for

metaphor a figure of speech in which a word or phrase is applied to an object, a character or an action which does not literally belong to it, in order to imply a resemblance and create an unusual or striking image in the reader's mind

metre the rhythmic arrangement of syllables in poetic verse

metrical foot a group of two or more syllables in which one of the syllables has the major stress. The basic unit of poetic rhythm

narrative a story, tale or any recital of events, and the manner in which it is told. First person narratives ('I') are told from the character's perspective and usually require the reader to judge carefully what is being said; second person narratives ('you') suggest the reader is part of the story; in third person narratives ('he, 'she', 'they') the narrator may be intrusive (continually commenting on the story), impersonal, or omniscient. More than one style of narrative may be used in a text

narrator the voice telling the story or relating a sequence of events

ode a serious lyric poem celebrating a particular event or subject

oxymoron a figure of speech in which words with contradictory meanings are brought together for effect

persona(e) the use of an imagined character as the voice or speaker of a poem

personification the treatment or description of an object or an idea as human, with human attributes and feelings

quadrameter line of verse with four metrical feet

rhetorical devices figures of speech based on rhetoric – the art of persuasive speaking

Romantics Followers of a movement in the arts which reacted to the rationalist Age of Enlightenment and the Industrial Revolution, emphasising individualism, the power of nature, social equality and the irrational

satire a type of literature in which folly, evil or topical issues are held up to scorn through ridicule, irony or exaggeration

simile a figure of speech which compares two things using the words 'like' or 'as'

sonnet a poem of 14 lines, usually in two parts, an octet and a sextet, with a definite rhyme scheme, normally in **iambic pentameter**

spondee a verse foot consisting of a pair of stressed syllables

stanza in a poem, when lines of verse are grouped together into units, these units are called stanzas. They usually follow a pattern with a fixed number of lines and a set number of **metrical feet** within each line

symbolism investing material objects with abstract powers and meanings greater than their own; allowing a complex idea to be represented by a single object

synecdoche making a part of something stand for the whole

syntax the grammatical way in which words combine to create meaning

tetrameter metre consisting of four feet per line

trochee a verse foot consisting of a stressed syllable followed by an unstressed

Victorian a term referring to the reign of Queen Victoria (1837–1901). It was a time of huge change in society, outlook and literary output, with the Industrial Revolution transforming life in the cities and the countryside, and the conservative status quo challenged by new thinking in the realms of religion and politics

Steve Eddy graduated from the University of Warwick with an honours degree in English and American Literature. He has taught English at secondary level and is the author of numerous English text books and GCSE and A Level literature study guides. These include guides to several Shakespeare plays, Thomas Hardy, John Steinbeck and Mildred Taylor, and YNA titles on William Golding's *The Spire* and Philip Larkin's *High Windows*. He has also published a number of books on mythology.

NOTES

NOTES

GCSE

Maya Angelou
I Know Why the Caged Bird Sings

Jane Austen
Pride and Prejudice

Alan Ayckbourn
Absent Friends

Elizabeth Barrett Browning
Selected Poems

Robert Bolt
A Man for All Seasons

Harold Brighouse
Hobson's Choice

Charlotte Brontë
Jane Eyre

Emily Brontë
Wuthering Heights

Brian Clark
Whose Life is it Anyway?

Robert Cormier
Heroes

Shelagh Delaney
A Taste of Honey

Charles Dickens
David Copperfield
Great Expectations
Hard Times
Oliver Twist
Selected Stories

Roddy Doyle
Paddy Clarke Ha Ha Ha

George Eliot
Silas Marner
The Mill on the Floss

Anne Frank
The Diary of a Young Girl

William Golding
Lord of the Flies

Oliver Goldsmith
She Stoops to Conquer

Willis Hall
The Long and the Short and the Tall

Thomas Hardy
Far from the Madding Crowd
The Mayor of Casterbridge
Tess of the d'Urbervilles
The Withered Arm and other Wessex Tales

L. P. Hartley
The Go-Between

Seamus Heaney
Selected Poems

Susan Hill
I'm the King of the Castle

Barry Hines
A Kestrel for a Knave

Louise Lawrence
Children of the Dust

Harper Lee
To Kill a Mockingbird

Laurie Lee
Cider with Rosie

Arthur Miller
The Crucible
A View from the Bridge

Robert O'Brien
Z for Zachariah

Frank O'Connor
My Oedipus Complex and Other Stories

George Orwell
Animal Farm

J. B. Priestley
An Inspector Calls
When We Are Married

Willy Russell
Educating Rita
Our Day Out

J. D. Salinger
The Catcher in the Rye

William Shakespeare
Henry IV Part I
Henry V
Julius Caesar
Macbeth
The Merchant of Venice
A Midsummer Night's Dream
Much Ado About Nothing
Romeo and Juliet
The Tempest
Twelfth Night

George Bernard Shaw
Pygmalion

Mary Shelley
Frankenstein

R. C. Sherriff
Journey's End

Rukshana Smith
Salt on the Snow

John Steinbeck
Of Mice and Men

Robert Louis Stevenson
Dr Jekyll and Mr Hyde

Jonathan Swift
Gulliver's Travels

Robert Swindells
Daz 4 Zoe

Mildred D. Taylor
Roll of Thunder, Hear My Cry

Mark Twain
Huckleberry Finn

James Watson
Talking in Whispers

Edith Wharton
Ethan Frome

William Wordsworth
Selected Poems

A Choice of Poets

Mystery Stories of the Nineteenth Century including The Signalman

Nineteenth Century Short Stories

Poetry of the First World War

Six Women Poets

For the AQA Anthology:

Duffy and Armitage & Pre-1914 Poetry

Heaney and Clarke & Pre-1914 Poetry

Poems from Different Cultures

Key Stage 3

William Shakespeare
Henry V
Macbeth
Much Ado About Nothing
Richard III
The Tempest

Margaret Atwood
Cat's Eye
The Handmaid's Tale

Jane Austen
Emma
Mansfield Park
Persuasion
Pride and Prejudice
Sense and Sensibility

William Blake
Songs of Innocence and of Experience

The Brontës
Selected Poems

Charlotte Brontë
Jane Eyre
Villette

Emily Brontë
Wuthering Heights

Angela Carter
The Bloody Chamber
Nights at the Circus
Wise Children

Geoffrey Chaucer
The Franklin's Prologue and Tale
The Merchant's Prologue and Tale
The Miller's Prologue and Tale
The Pardoner's Tale
The Prologue to the Canterbury Tales
The Wife of Bath's Prologue and Tale

Caryl Churchill
Top Girls

John Clare
Selected Poems

Joseph Conrad
Heart of Darkness

Charles Dickens
Bleak House
Great Expectations
Hard Times

Emily Dickinson
Selected Poems

Carol Ann Duffy
Selected Poems
The World's Wife

George Eliot
Middlemarch
The Mill on the Floss

T. S. Eliot
Selected Poems
The Waste Land

F. Scott Fitzgerald
The Great Gatsby

John Ford
'Tis Pity She's a Whore

E. M. Forster
A Passage to India

Michael Frayn
Spies

Charles Frazier
Cold Mountain

Brian Friel
Making History
Translations

William Golding
The Spire

Thomas Hardy
Jude the Obscure
The Mayor of Casterbridge
The Return of the Native
Selected Poems
Tess of the d'Urbervilles

Seamus Heaney
Selected Poems from 'Opened Ground'

Nathaniel Hawthorne
The Scarlet Letter

Homer
The Iliad
The Odyssey

Aldous Huxley
Brave New World

Henrik Ibsen
A Doll's House

Kazuo Ishiguro
The Remains of the Day

James Joyce
Dubliners

John Keats
Selected Poems

Philip Larkin
High Windows
The Whitsun Weddings and Selected Poems

Ian McEwan
Atonement

Christopher Marlowe
Doctor Faustus
Edward II

Arthur Miller
All My Sons
Death of a Salesman

John Milton
Paradise Lost Books I & II

Toni Morrison
Beloved

George Orwell
Nineteen Eighty-Four

Sylvia Plath
Selected Poems

William Shakespeare
Antony and Cleopatra
As You Like It
Hamlet
Henry IV Part I
King Lear
Macbeth
Measure for Measure
The Merchant of Venice
A Midsummer Night's Dream
Much Ado About Nothing
Othello
Richard II
Richard III
Romeo and Juliet
The Taming of the Shrew
The Tempest
Twelfth Night
The Winter's Tale

Mary Shelley
Frankenstein

Richard Brinsley Sheridan
The School for Scandal

Bram Stoker
Dracula

Alfred Tennyson
Selected Poems

Alice Walker
The Color Purple

John Webster
The Duchess of Malfi
The White Devil

Oscar Wilde
The Importance of Being Earnest
A Woman of No Importance

Tennessee Williams
Cat on a Hot Tin Roof
The Glass Menagerie
A Streetcar Named Desire

Jeanette Winterson
Oranges Are Not the Only Fruit

Virginia Woolf
To the Lighthouse

William Wordsworth
The Prelude and Selected Poems

W. B. Yeats
Selected Poems
Poetry of the First World War